ON THE LAND

*American Agriculture
from Past to Present*

ON THE LAND

*American Agriculture
from Past to Present*

illustrated with photographs

ELINOR LANDER HORWITZ

A Margaret K. McElderry Book

Atheneum   1980   *New York*

Library of Congress catalog card number 79-3545
ISBN 0-689-50165-X
Copyright © 1980 by Elinor Lander Horwitz
All rights reserved
·Manufactured by Halliday Lithograph Corporation
West Hanover, Massachusetts
Designed by Maria Epes
First Edition

For my father
who would have preferred being a farmer

CONTENTS

I   *The Price of Plenty*   7

II   *Beginning the World Anew*   21

III   *The Farm Worker*   33

IV   *The Public Domain*   49

V   *The Start of the Modern Era*   63

VI   *Boom and Bust*   82

VII   *Where We Stand*   101

VIII   *Can We Save the Family Farm?*   113

Suggestions for Further Reading   131

Index   133

In the early years of our nationhood, when nine out of ten Americans were engaged in agriculture, Thomas Jefferson wrote, "The small landholders are the most precious part of the state." In Jefferson's view the farmers and their families were the most "independent" and "virtuous" of all citizens, "tied to their country and wedded to its liberty and interests by the most lasting bonds." Along with many other philosophizers, most of them uninvolved in the daily toil of crop production, Jefferson extolled agriculture as a divine calling in which the farmer joined in partnership with the deity to nourish mankind. "Those who labor on the earth," he wrote, "are the chosen people of God."

Today, although only 4.5 percent of Americans are engaged in farming, farmers as a group are still highly esteemed. In language considerably less eloquent than Jefferson's, a recent Department of Agriculture survey revealed that most of us believe that farm families work longer and harder than people in other occupations and that, unlike city dwellers, they are "friendly and helpful." Most of us automatically endow someone from a rural background with special virtue. We are pleased to discover that a new friend, a teacher, our doctor or dentist was raised on a farm. We trust a political candidate who —knowing of our bias—refers often and with nostalgic pleasure to those days when, as a boy, he rose at five each morning to milk the cows.

Most farmers themselves respond in the affirmative when asked by pollsters if they consider farming a satisfying way of life. But when asked if they would like to see their children

Appalachian farm, Leslie County, Kentucky, 1978. ANTHONY HORWITZ
(following page)

follow in their footsteps, they express hopes tempered by pessimism. Farming, they say, is an admirable way of life but an almost hopeless way of making a living.

The fact that dawn to dusk labors have in most cases brought "the chosen people of God" very little reward in the form of income was, until this century, accepted as appropriate. Farming was a way of life. Until the middle of the nineteenth century only a very few large-scale commercial farmers and ranchers viewed agriculture as a business enterprise. The average farmer raised crops and livestock to feed and clothe his family, enjoying a life of independence and self-sufficiency. All family members worked in the fields and in the home growing, harvesting, and preserving food, carding and spinning wool, weaving cloth, making clothing, repairing equipment and household goods. Neighbors helped each other with the construction of houses and barns, and such necessities as coffee, tea, and sugar, which could not be grown at home, could be obtained from the local shopkeeper by barter.

Today the contemporary farm family shops at the supermarket and the department store, buys television sets, air conditioners, trucks and tractors, pays for insurance, medical care, college tuitions, and vacation trips. If farming is to survive as a way of life, it must also succeed as a business venture.

Can the man Jefferson dubbed "the most precious part of the state" be saved? Is it in our national interest that he *be* saved? What is being done to help the small and medium-sized farmer in his struggle to stay on the land? How did a nation of small landholders become a country in which over one hundred thousand farm families are forced each year to abandon the land?

CHAPTER I
The Price of Plenty

In the past four decades an agricultural revolution has taken place in this country based on an unprecedented expansion of technology, particularly in the area of mechanization. Whereas in 1940 there were 6 million farms and a farm labor force of 11 million people, today we have only 2.7 million farms worked by 4 million people. Average farm size has increased during that period from 175 acres to over 400 acres and the largest 2 percent of farms account for 37 percent of sales.

What these basic statistics reveal is a trend toward larger and fewer farms, which we have every reason to believe will continue. As production nationwide has steadily increased, the small farmer has been less and less able to compete. Profitable agriculture now requires a high level of both technological and managerial know-how and enormous outlays of capital. As farmers with small or medium-sized holdings sell out, their land is taken over by developers—or more often by wealthier neighboring farmers who are expanding their acreage and production assisted by government programs. Since farming has traditionally required long hours of repetitive exhausting toil, the fact that the mechanization of agriculture has "released" millions of farmers from the necessity of working on the land, while consumers enjoy a super-abundance of relatively inexpensive food, is often cited as irrefutable evidence of progress. It has been considered a matter of national pride that, despite rising prices, Americans spend less than a fifth of their income on food, a smaller percentage than people of any other nation; that one farmer with modern machinery can now do virtually all the work to grow 1,000 acres of corn or 2,000 acres of wheat; that

7

one man working in a mechanized broiler raising operation can tend 70,000 chicks.

There is no question about the fact that the quantity and diversity of our agricultural output is unequalled in history. The average farm worker in this country feeds fifty-two people, and the harvest from one in every three acres is sent abroad. Our farms are producing more food and fiber than the most visionary agriculturist of earlier generations imagined to be possible —but this bounty has not come to us without social and environmental costs and cause for grave concern about the future.

What we refer to as "The Farm Problem" is actually many interwoven problems—a complex economic, human, ecological, and social issue that has come about through decades and centuries of ever-increasing agricultural production. For a constantly growing number of small and medium-sized farmers, the basic concern is that our country's historic concentration on productivity has led to oversupply and low farm income. As the cost of operating a farm continues to rise, our farm population is decreasing rapidly, and two-thirds of the remaining farmers and their families now earn the major part of their income from off-farm jobs. Although a great many young people cherish the goal of farm ownership, the high cost of land and equipment has made this ideal unobtainable to all but a few.

Today not only the farmer but people from all areas of public and private life are questioning our confidence in the belief that ever expanding productivity equals progress and success. They see the family farm and our once-healthy rural economy severely threatened. They are concerned as consumers about the wholesomeness of the food grown by big-business agriculture and about the ecological damage caused by modern farming methods. They have grown sharply critical of the "efficiency" of modern agricultural technology, in which it has become more profitable to use toxic chemicals than natural fertilizer and biological means of pest control and high energy consuming machines rather than people. The plight of our most exploited citizens, the migratory farm workers, is a source of deep concern to many. Government programs that promote farm technology suitable only to large-scale operations are being scrutinized and attacked by public interest groups, Con-

Settlers from Bendon, Minnesota, at the Sun River, Hancock Home-stead, 1910. UNITED STATES DEPARTMENT OF AGRICULTURE

gressional committees, and an increasingly vocal public.

The eighteenth century economist Adam Smith had little confidence that agriculture would progress as efficiently as manufacturing. Unlike manufacturing, where different functions can be performed by different people working simultaneously, in farming, he wrote, "One man cannot always be ploughing, another sowing, and another reaping . . . a worker who only practiced one agricultural operation would lie idle eleven months of the year."

In fact, if we accept the amount produced per worker per hour as the sole measure of efficiency, agriculture has surpassed manufacturing. The output of the industrial laborer has increased one and a half times in the past twenty years whereas that of the agricultural worker has tripled. What Smith could not foresee is that many farming activities would be taken over by specialized machines that plowed, seeded, cultivated, and harvested, and that could be run twenty-four hours a day when necessary. He could not have imagined that abundant tomato harvests would be gathered by mechanical harvesters equipped with electronic eyes that sort green tomatoes from red ones. He could not have imagined that, since tomatoes are by nature fragile and machines by design are iron-clawed, a new tough-skinned tomato would be developed that could be picked mechanically. And he could scarcely have foreseen that consumers would cheerfully pay through their tax dollars for this type of research and would willingly buy and eat the new untasty tomatoes; that 32,000 picking jobs in California would be lost to people critically in need of employment; and that 85 percent of the state's farmers, who grew tomatoes for canning purposes, would not be able to compete by buying their own $25,000 to $40,000 harvesting machines and would be forced off the land.

In California, which leads the country in the production of a great many of our most commonly consumed fruits and vegetables, most of the crops that go to freezing or canning processors are now picked by machine. Lettuce, table grapes, and a number of other tender fruits and vegetables sold fresh in foodstores are usually still hand picked, but new machines are being developed to harvest wine grapes, lettuce, broccoli, as-

10

paragus, olives, and other crops. Citrus fruits are hand picked also, although 85 percent of California oranges go to processors.

Until 1970 most fruits and vegetables even on the largest factory-type farms were still gathered by migrant families, who follow the harvest from south to north, traveling in rundown buses, sheltering in camps notorious for their squalor erected by large growers at minimal cost for people too helpless in their poverty to object.

Efforts to improve wages and living conditions for the farm-workers have, in turn, speeded research in mechanization. Thousands of migratory pickers are replaced each year by machines and most become welfare clients. The use of public resources for this research is usually justified by claims that savings in production costs will keep food prices down. Critics point out that since the mechanization of the tomato harvest in 1965, canned vegetables as a group have risen 76 percent in price by 1980, while canned tomatoes have risen 111 percent, with increased profits from mechanization going to processors rather than consumers. Research that resulted in the tough-skinned tomato also introduced methods for turning green tomatoes red—but not ripe—with ethylene gas, techniques for removing fuzz from peaches and coating them with wax containing fungicides that would prolong their life in storage, and other innovations that have made our food less wholesome.

Modern technology that requires a high expenditure of energy, which we have encouraged not only at home but around the world, has made U.S. agriculture, in the words of former Secretary of Agriculture Earl Butz, "the number one customer of the petroleum industry." Today, when our ability to survive on this planet must be measured in terms of energy resources, the question is posed as to whether fuel shortages will some day lead to food shortages.

Energy input into food production, processing, distribution, and preparation for consumption begins with the use of planting, cultivating, irrigating, and harvesting equipment. As the equipment has increased in size and effectiveness, escalating energy use has resulted. But fueling agricultural machinery and the trucks, trains, and planes that link the grower to the consumer are only part of the energy picture. Our increasingly

11

controversial chemical pesticides and fertilizers consume huge quantities of fossil fuel both in their production and in their composition. Over 90 percent of chemical fertilizers are made from natural gas. Pesticides are formulated on petroleum-based solvents.

For this reason, and for public health reasons, the pesticide issue is a major concern in any discussion of today's agricultural scene. The chemicals commonly used have polluted the water and the air, damaged mockingbirds as well as mites, invaded our body tissues and the once-pure driven snow. Acute pesticide contamination has caused death among farmworkers and long-range low-level exposure has been implicated in miscarriages and the birth of children with neurological impairments. Insecticides and herbicides have caused cancer and birth defects in laboratory animals. All of which is not really surprising. After all, a pesticide is simply a poison—a poison we can spray into the air and onto the food we eat. As Alice in Wonderland commented to the white rabbit, "If you drink very much from a bottle marked POISON, it's almost certain to disagree with you sooner or later."

Developed during World War II as a health agent, DDT, a chlorinated hydrocarbon, was greeted as "the miracle bug killer" when it was introduced for agricultural pest control in the 1940s. Used to halt insect-transmitted diseases such as malaria, typhus, and encephalitis, the chemical saved millions of people around the world from suffering and death. DDT, which could be applied as a spray, a dust, or a dip, which could be spread on fields and swamps from airplanes or dispensed in suburban gardens from small hand-held containers, was seen as the ultimate weapon in the eternal battle farmers wage to save their crops from destruction by insect invasion. However, in the 1960s, DDT and a number of similar compounds were banned from routine agricultural use by the Environmental Protection Agency, which has also placed two thousand compounds considered "potentially hazardous" on a restricted list. But newer chemicals continue to appear on the market and have created and continue to create a host of complex problems. Pesticide production is now a 3.5 billion dollar a year industry, and evaluating the safety of pesticides has become a

Spraying cotton with DDT near Lubbock, Texas, 1950. UNITED STATES
DEPARTMENT OF AGRICULTURE

major governmental concern. Their production in the United States has climbed to 1.6 billion pounds annually from 200,000 pounds in 1950, when the dangers of pesticide use were unrecognized. To date, however, there has been little monitoring of farm products for excessive pesticide application and little action against violations of pesticide use restrictions. Responsibility for regulation is divided among the Department of Agriculture, the Food and Drug Administration, and the Environmental Protection Agency. Authorities and methods of inspection and enforcement vary among all three and there are limited technical and legal means for protecting consumers from contaminated produce, meat, and poultry.

Ironically, it was the qualities that made DDT such an exciting product in the 1940s that later were recognized as dangerous. DDT works fast and its effects are persistent, making it an efficient bug killer all season long and equally deadly to a broad spectrum of pests. Rachel Carson, in her perceptive book, *Silent Spring,* published in 1962, alerted the public to the effects of pesticides on the reproductive capacity of birds and other wildlife. It was discovered that DDT persisted in the earth, in the water, and in animal tissue, moving with the food-chain to invade the tissues of higher animals, including man. Because it attacked a wide range of organisms, it was killing off not only target pests but also their natural enemies, pollinating insects, and other essential species. A particularly damaging "asset" was that DDT was low-priced, which to a large extent accounted for its overuse. Farmers, who gleaned their information from salesmen and from labels, began applying pesticides for prevention as well as for cure with no concern for side-effects. As pesticide use increased so did insect resistance, so more and more DDT was used.

Today 364 species of insects, mites, and ticks in the world are resistant to one or more chemical pesticides. Malaria-transmitting mosquitoes, as an example, are no longer affected by DDT and other insecticides. The response has been to use more pesticides than ever before. Although usage has increased ten times since the 1940s, agricultural losses to insects and plant diseases have increased over the past decade from 31.4 percent

14

in 1942 to 33 percent in 1974. Post-harvest losses of stored food to microorganisms, insects, and rodents bring total losses to 39 percent in this country, where pesticide use is higher than anywhere else in the world.

Herbicides, introduced at the same time as DDT, are chemicals that kill weeds formerly controlled on crop land and along highways, power lines, and rights of way by cultivation. Farmers found the new herbicides worked with amazing speed and effectiveness, eliminating the need for tedious tillage of such areas. But, like pesticides, many herbicides are now banned or limited in use because they have been implicated in genetic, reproductive, or neurological damage or are considered carcinogenic.

Veterans of the Vietnam War have recently instituted class action law suits claiming that a range of severe health problems they have suffered since the war can be traced to exposure to the herbicide, Agent Orange, which was used to destroy the enemy's food supply and tree cover in large areas of Vietnam. One component of Agent Orange—the name refers to the orange colored containers in which it was stored—was the recently banned herbicide 2,4,5-T, which contains dioxin, one of the most deadly chemicals known.

There is an alternative to pest control programs based on exclusive use of chemical pesticides. It is known as IPM or Integrated Pest Management. IPM techniques seek to combine some use of chemical pesticides with other biological and environmental controls to achieve a pest management plan that protects people, other animals, and the environment. Natural controls, such as introducing predators, diseases, and parasites, and altering insect behavior or physiology are basic techniques. Scientists have discovered how to sythesize sex attractants emitted by female insects. Through release of these synthetic substances males are lured, entrapped, and either sterilized and then set loose, or they are destroyed.

Combined with such methods there is, as well, a return to soil tillage, crop rotation, and the introduction of disease and pest resistant species of plants. Starting at the turn of the century, geneticists experimented with controlled breeding

15

programs to select disease and pest-resistant crop varieties. In recent decades most breeding programs have been centered on developing new high-yield, uniformly maturing crops suitable for machine harvesting—crops that also have eye-appeal at the supermarket. Now attention is being directed toward developing varieties that can be grown with low pesticide use. Although monoculture—large areas devoted to a single crop—is particularly profitable today because farmers can fully utilize highly specialized machinery, the potential for crop epidemics is seriously increased when one variety is extended over a large area. It was this type of agriculture that led to the Irish potato famine in the 1840s, when the potato crop was destroyed.

Although only 1.1 percent of the U.S. Department of Agriculture's budget for 1979 went to IPM research, examples of successful use of IPM techniques are impressive. The Hessian fly, a grave concern soon after the Revolutionary War, when it was first seen in this country, has been a serious threat to wheat crops ever since. Recently it has been brought under control by the introduction of natural enemies and by planting resistant varieties of wheat. The klamath weed has been controlled by leaf beetles, introduced from Australia. Weeds that threatened rice fields have been controlled by altering flooding schedules. Red scale, a citrus pest, has been brought under control by a beetle and a fly, which are its natural enemies; sugar cane pests by several predator insects and a fungus. Herbs have been planted that repel certain kinds of flies, moths, and mosquitoes. Synthesized sex attractants or pheromones have been released to lure the European fruit fly away from the crops. A project in Texas has shown that with IPM techniques cotton can be raised at an increased profit with 50 to 75 percent less insecticide, 80 percent less fertilizer, and 50 percent less irrigation than previously used.

Pesticide use is not wholly abandoned under IPM but is employed specifically to keep pest populations from reaching excessive levels. Heavy use of chemicals is still recommended against foreign pests when they are first noted in this country, in hopes that their populations can be kept so low that they will not become established here.

Many of the biological controls are used without pesticides in organic gardening techniques. Although the term "organically grown" is not always precisely defined, it generally indicates that crops have been raised without the use of synthetic pesticides or fertilizers. Organic farmers use compost, manure, nitrogen-fixing crops such as legumes, and other natural materials to feed the soil. It is difficult to evaluate claims that organically grown food is more vitamin-laden than food grown by other methods, but as the public becomes increasingly concerned about chemical residues and less concerned with minor blemishes on fruits and vegetables, the market for organically grown produce has expanded. Very few agricultural schools, however, encourage organic farming or offer courses in the subject at this time.

The resistance of most farmers to the use of natural fertilizers and biological methods of pest control is based on the fact that chemicals are so easily handled, stored, and applied, and are fast acting. There is no question, however, that water pollution results from the runoff of highly soluble chemical fertilizers into streams, rivers, and lakes. Although such fertilizers are increasingly expensive because of the high price of fuel used in their manufacture, they have been excessively applied, particularly on corn, cotton, wheat, and soybeans. Fertilizer use nationwide has increased 500 percent since World War II.

Natural fertilizers can also cause pollution. Contemporary methods of confining tens of thousands of cattle on vast feed lots lead to rapid accumulation of manure, which often runs off into streams and rivers. When animals and crops were tended on the same land it was easy and economical to recycle animal wastes, rejected today by most farmers in favor of chemical fertilizers, which are easier to store and to use. Contemporary confinement methods of raising cattle and poultry have led to other problems as well. Because close confinement —laying hens are now restricted to one-third of a square foot of cage space—lowers animal resistance to disease, cattle, broiler chickens, and laying hens are now given hormones and antibiotics both to prevent illness and to increase weight gain while cutting feed requirements. We know that DES (Diethylstil-

17

besterol), a female hormone frequently used, can cause cancer in test animals, and there is concern about what happens to consumers who later eat these products. Organic gardeners dub meat and poultry "organically raised," to indicate that their nurturing did not allow the use of hormones and antibiotics.

Contemporary agricultural technology has also been implicated in land abuse which, unlike the pesticide issue, is hardly a new problem. The history of soil degradation in this country goes back to the tobacco and cotton farmers of the seventeenth century. It was most dramatically demonstrated in this century by the careless farming methods that led to severe wind erosion and dust storms in the 1930s. Dust storms also damaged areas of the Great Plains in 1977 causing severe hardships to local farmers. In southern Florida vegetables are grown by large corporate farms in drained wetland soils that are oxidizing so rapidly that they are expected to have completely disappeared by the year 2000. Peat soils when covered with water are protected from oxygen. When they are drained the organic materials in peat combine with the oxygen in the air and decay occurs rapidly. A strong case against the large industrial corporate farm is that the investor, unlike the small farmer who hopes to pass his land on to his children, is interested only in short-term economic gains and has little concern with preserving the soil for the use and profit of the next generation.

A recent U.S. Department of Agriculture (USDA) survey shows that 64 percent of our crop lands are in need of conservation measures. The Soil Conservation Service has reported that over two billion tons of soil were washed from crop lands in 1977 and three billion tons were blown away by wind. Loss of soil is attributed to planting crops on marginal land, which erodes easily, to lack of crop rotation, which began when the use of chemical fertilizers became widespread, to the use of huge machines, which have obliterated the old methods of plowing and planting in terraces, and to discarding old practices of letting land rest under grass or legume crops, which protect the soil.

Our current understanding of the natural world is quite different from that of the nineteenth century farmer, who

18

never questioned the importance of making every acre of land produce. Guided by this philosophy, which was also official governmental policy, swamps were drained and forests cleared and grasslands plowed. The first conservation measures began in the 1890s, after the closing of the frontier, when timberland was put in reserve under President Grover Cleveland for the first time despite the opinion of Speaker of the House Joseph Cannon, who evoked a sympathetic response when he asked, "Why should I do anything for posterity? What has posterity done for me?" Under Theodore Roosevelt's leadership, however, more timberland was put in reserve than under all preceding administrations. The first reclamation program was the 1902 National Reclamation Act which inaugurated government action in the irrigation of arid western lands. Although the Mormons had successfully diverted water from City Creek near the present site of Salt Lake City to grow a large variety of crops as early as 1847, before 1902 other irrigation projects were always accomplished by individuals, cooperatives, and commercial companies.

Today we no longer think of our natural resources as boundless and inexhaustible. Helping farmers to conserve their farmland is now a priority of government policy. United States cropland totals 400 million acres of which about two million acres a year are being converted to non-agricultural use. A new concern about agricultural land availability is the growing number of people who consider farmland a good investment. Their motivation for land use differs from that of the traditional farmer. Forty-three states have enacted legislation designed to retain agricultural land. In addition to loss of crop-production capacity, loss of open land to residential, commercial, or industrial development also has broad implications for the maintenance of groundwater supplies.

Recent government programs, such as the Food and Agriculture Act of 1977, combine price support programs with conservation by ruling that land formerly used for crops and now taken out of production must be devoted to conservation uses or wildlife habitat. Other conservation cost-sharing programs and pollution control programs to conserve cropland and im-

19

prove water quality are administered by the Department of Agriculture, the Environmental Protection Agency, the Small Business Administration, and the Farmer's Home Administration. Ironically government programs, such as home mortgage guarantees, highways, and other public works often press in the opposite direction by encouraging urban sprawl or irreversibly committing prime land to non-agricultural uses.

CHAPTER II

Beginning the World Anew

In the early eighteenth century Jonathan Swift wrote, "Whoever could make two ears of corn or two blades of grass to grow upon a spot of ground where only one grew before would deserve better of mankind and do more essential service to this country than the whole race of politicians put together." He was enthusiastically quoted by the first United States Commissioner of Agriculture, Isaac Newton, who in 1863 announced that, "It should be the aim of every young farmer to do not only as well as his father but to do his best: to make two blades of grass grow where but one grew before."

Our extraordinary success in making more and more blades of grass grow where one grew before has led not only to unprecedented agricultural production but to severe problems of surplus disposal and low farm income. If the ghosts of the Jamestown or Plymouth settlers could hear the news that agricultural overproduction has become a major economic and political issue they would find it incomprehensible. In their day agricultural abundance was a treasured distant dream and subsistence a most vital immediate goal. They defined the farm problem very simply: inadequate agricultural production would lead to starvation. The territory that would become the United States was occupied by approximately a million Indians who spent the major part of their time and energy providing food for themselves. When the Pilgrims and their Indian guests feasted on stringy turkey and tough corn and unsweetened cranberries for three days of thanksgiving after gathering their meager harvest in the autumn of 1621 they were celebrating the most basic triumph of all—the miracle of their survival.

21

The first settlers to arrive in this country from the crowded cities and towns of Europe found a vast untamed land—a land of dense primeval forests laced with narrow, barely passable Indian trails. Patches of clearings where the Indians grew their crops had been observed earlier by sixteenth and seventeenth century explorers, but otherwise the entire eastern part of the country was a virtually impenetrable woodland. As one astonished seventeenth century arrival wrote to friends back in the old world, "The whole country is a perfect forest!"

Jared Eliot, whose *Essays Upon Field Husbandry* was the first book on farming published in this country, wrote a century later of these refugees from European civilization: "When we consider the small number of the first Settlers, and coming from an Old Cultivated Country, to thick Woods, rough unimproved Landes; where all their former Experience and Knowledge was now of very little Service to them. . . It may be said, that in a Sort, they began the World a New."

Beginning the world anew involved, most urgently, clearing land for cultivation. From the Indians, who had no metal tools, no wheeled carts, and no draft animals, the settlers learned a neolithic method known as girdling, in which the death of a tree was caused by interrupting the flow of water and nutrients to the branches. With stone implements, the Indians cut a deep ring around the tree trunks and stripped away the bark. In the spring they grew corn and other vegetables in the sunlit areas under the leafless trees, removing the smaller branches with sharp stone axes.

The difficulties of farming the rough terrain, once the trees had been killed, were compounded by the fact that so many of the settlers were city and townspeople with little knowledge of agriculture. And although the new world was rich in game, few of the settlers were skilled in the use of the clumsy rifles of the period, since hunting in Europe was a sport available only to the gentry. The fact that any of the Plymouth colonists survived the first particularly difficult years was due entirely to the assistance of the Indians, who had developed crops and farming methods suitable to local conditions.

The Plymouth settlers were assisted by the Indian Squanto of the Pawtuxet tribe who showed them how to burn off the

Clearing a homestead out of the wilderness. NATIONAL ARCHIVES.

growth of weeds in some partially cleared and abandoned Indian fields and to plant their corn in holes filled with dead herring that had been trapped in brooks during their spring migration. As the dead fish decomposed they gave off nitrogen, fertilizing the cornfield. The settlers timed their planting according to the Indian rule, which dictated that corn must go into the ground when the new leaves on the oak trees reached the size of a mouse's ear.

Thirteen years before the *Mayflower* arrived in Plymouth, there had been winters of starvation in the first permanent English settlement at Jamestown. Although the Jamestown settlement was well located for shipping and defense, the marshy ground was far from ideal for farming and disputes over land halted trade with the Indians. It was not until instruction was given the settlers by two Indian captives that some limited level of crop production was attained. In 1610 new arrivals found a small group of half-starved colonists, most of whom were living on oysters, snakes, roots, acorns, and wild fruit.

During the next decade, conditions improved considerably and what were referred to as "the starving years" became a fearful memory and a lasting admonition. Ships from England brought over chickens, pigs, goats, and sheep. The marriage of Pocohontas and John Rolfe brought peace between the British and the Indians, and tobacco, the all-American crop, which the settlers learned to grow from the Indians, became a valuable export. In both the southern and the northern colonies Indian corn or maize provided the mainstay of diet, and despite all the changes in agricultural production that have occurred since, corn is still today our most valuable single crop.

Among the Indians, planting and cultivating crops was the job of the women, children, and old people of the tribe, although the tobacco fields were tended by the men. Unplowed land was broken up with a hoe made by lashing a sharp stone or the shoulder blade of a deer or moose to a wooden handle. Large clamshells, also often tied to a handle, were used for weeding. Corn was planted in hills located about three feet apart. When the stalks began to grow, beans were planted nearby and their vines would climb the supporting stalks.

The self-sufficient colonial farmer, who used methods only slightly less primitive than those of the native inhabitants, made most of his own implements, going to the village blacksmith when he needed someone to hammer out a hoe blade or an axe. Iron hoes, spades, shovels, and scythes were brought from Europe, but even after the first plows arrived and, later, oxen to pull them, farming practices remained similar to those of two millennia earlier and changed little during the next two centuries.

The first plows used here were so large and cumbersome that teams of four to six oxen were required to move them along the glacial soil of New England. One man walked behind the plow keeping a firm grip on the handles and a second man pressed downwards on the beam so that the plow would dig into the ground. A third man had the job of removing the soil that stuck to the moldboard, the rotating piece behind the point of the plow, which turns the earth. A young boy could take on the fourth essential job—that of leading the animals in a straight line. Plowing an acre, even to a shallow depth, was a full day's work. Since plows remained uncommon during the first half-century of settlement, work was most often done by itinerant plowmen who bartered their services for crops.

The life of the seventeenth century American farm family was at best arduous, perilous, and austere. Indian raids and bloody reprisals began soon after settlement in both northern and southern colonies and continued through 1763. Invariably they concerned disputes over land, which the Indians considered sacred and indivisible and which the colonists had acquired through capture or barter or royal grants of dubious validity. The diet of the early settlers was based on the abundant corn harvests, and a mush of cornmeal and water was served as a porridge or baked into cakes and eaten three times a day. Apples were abundant and cider soon became the most common drink. Corn and beans were dried and preserved through the winter without loss of food value and as the years passed salt pork and bacon were common fare. In the eighteenth century the range of crops increased rapidly as new settlers brought every fruit and vegetable grown in Europe, but in

Man using ox-drawn wooden plow in Greene County, Georgia, 1941.
LIBRARY OF CONGRESS *(following page)*

the winter corn mush, corn cakes, corn bread, smoked or salted pork, milk and cider appeared on the table at every meal—and were eaten after giving thanks.

The colonists at first lived in rude shelters made of thatch or in wigwam-type dwellings of bent branches interlaced with reeds, which resembled the huts occupied by shepherds in Europe. Some settlers built sturdy cabins with squared logs, but they were tiny and windowless and had dirt floors. Despite their hard living conditions the first settlers in New England seem to have been a very hearty breed. Court records indicate that although most of the cattle and horses died of exposure during the early years, the colonists were long-lived. Men, women, and children all expected life to be a ceaseless round of hard work, and their complaints were reserved for the times when all their labor failed to achieve desired results.

In the South a successful commercial agriculture began early, with exports to Europe of tobacco, indigo, rice, and, in the eighteenth century, cotton. But if the New England farmer dreamed of becoming wealthy it was not to be through the sale of agricultural products but through commerce. Trade in furs and timber could be profitable. Some farmers became successful cod fishermen, and there was a market for salt fish, but sale of agricultural products was limited by difficulties in transportation. Seventeenth century roads were simply trails made by Indians and animals on which a man on a horse or a pack animal could barely pass. In the eighteenth century some of these roads were widened to accommodate the new carts and wagons, but most intercolonial trade moved by water and most settlements were located at seaports. Farmers in New York and Pennsylvania sent flour to New England and to Georgia and the Carolinas. By the mid-eighteenth century, when New England farms averaged forty acres, wheat farms in the Middle Colonies averaged 125 to 400 acres. Animal husbandry was also more advanced in the Middle Colonies where the German farmers, unlike the English colonists, routinely provided shelter and feed for livestock in winter. Philadelphia became a meat-packing and shipping center. Rice, tobacco, indigo, and sugar went from southern to northern ports, and farm products were sent north and south to feed people living on plantations entirely planted in tobacco. Ocean transport between England and America was the most profitable trade route although it took fifty to a hundred days or more going across, with the return voyage only fifteen to twenty-five days due to prevailing winds. Most ships had small cargo space and made no more than two round trips a year.

During the eighteenth century, as life grew more secure in the colonies, many visitors came from Europe to observe the curious customs of the New World. The American farmer became notorious for his wasteful land-use practices. In England farming was ruled by the so-called three-field system in which all the land under cultivation was divided into three large fields, one being left fallow each season in a rotating system. After the harvest the livestock were set loose in the fields to provide natural fertilization. In America, where land was available free for the taking west of the last settlement, exploitive practices were common in all the colonies. When topsoil was carried off by erosion after heavy storms or the land simply exhausted by lack of fertilization and overuse, new fields were brought under cultivation. Like the Indians, the colonists found it easier to clear new fields than to restore nutrients to depleted soil.

A Swedish professor of botany who toured the colonies in 1747 wrote, "After the inhabitants have converted into a tillable field a tract of land which was forest for many centuries and which consequently had a very fine soil, they use it as long as it will bear any crops. When it ceases to bear any they turn it into pastures for the cattle and take new grain fields in another place, where a rich black soil can be found that has never been used . . . Their eyes are fixed upon the present gain, and they are blind to the future."

Among the more enlightened agriculturists of the eighteenth century were George Washington and Thomas Jefferson, both intensely concerned husbandmen. Jefferson, on his farm at Monticello, set up a seven-year crop rotation system, advocated rotation to all farmers, strongly opposed single-crop farming, particularly when the crop was tobacco, which he felt ruined the soil. Already, poor agricultural practices were causing severe erosion, the topsoil washing into the streams and rivers which, in turn, silted up the harbors. Washington rotated tobacco, wheat, and forage on his extensive croplands at Mount Vernon and kept in touch with leading agriculturists in Europe. But the common man, who neither read agricultural treatises nor wished for advice, moved on.

Visitors to the New World were impressed by the American farmer's pride and independence, his industry and prosperity, compared to the peasants of the Old World. One visitor to a Connecticut farm family described the wagon that carried farm produce and supplies during the week and converted to a veritable coach on Sunday, with special detachable painted sides and hoops above supporting a decorated cloth covering. This wagon, he said, was capable of going seven miles per hour on roads from which the stumps had been removed. "I do not know where an American farmer can possibly enjoy more dignity as a father or as a citizen than when he thus carries with him his wife and family all clad in good, neat, homespun clothes, manufactured within his own house, and trots along with a neat pair of fat horses of his own raising."

As the American Revolution approached, frame dwellings and tidy homes of squared logs had become commonplace in well-settled areas. Farmers cooperated with neighbors to help gather the harvest and slaughter hogs and raise barns. Farm wives joined to make quilts, to shuck corn, to cook and bake for a sick neighbor. By the standards of the day the colonists ate well, but few had currency and most conducted business by barter. Lists were drawn up in townships showing the legal tender value of barley, oats, fish, butter—all commodities that could pay the minister's salary, the blacksmith's fee, a son's tuition at Harvard. Some local assemblies issued lists of farm products that could be used to pay taxes. In Pennsylvania and New York a farmer could buy services with vouchers for wheat.

In the South small family farms also predominated despite the fact that large plantations manned by slaves had established booming international trade in tobacco, cotton, indigo and rice.

Literacy was becoming more common and many men and

30

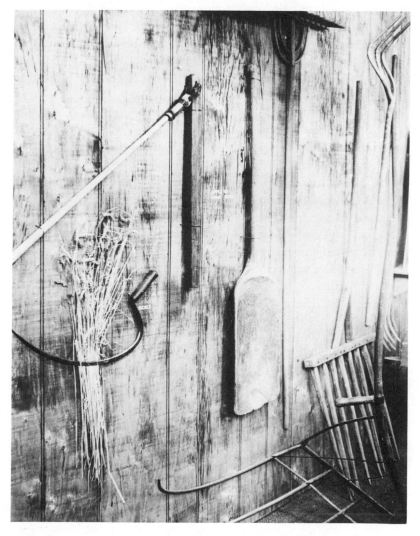

Early American farm implements. HERSHEY (PENNSYLVANIA) MUSEUM
OF AMERICAN LIFE

even some women could read from the Bible and write a little. A few other books were available. A farmer's son named Noah Webster became a country school teacher and wrote a spelling-book, reader, and grammar, and finally a dictionary. Jared Eliot's book on farming was followed by *The New England Farmer or Geographical Dictionary* by Samuel Deane, vice-president of Bowdoin College. Deane wrote regretfully of the fact that farming was a matter of such "hard and incessant labour," but felt that life was improving for those engaged in "the noblest employment" and that the day would come soon when "farmers shall toss about their dung with an air of majesty."

As the embattled farmers went off to fight in the Revolution a Rhode Island historian recorded that the women in his area gathered together to bring in the harvest, moving in a team from farm to farm. Although many fields became unproductive during the war and exports to Britain ceased, by and large American agriculture was stimulated by the coming of independence. Southern planters, who had turned their tobacco fields to grain during the war, returned to planting tobacco, and blockade runners carried the crop to Europe during the last two decades of the century. Indigo, which had been in great demand as a dye for the textile industries of England, was permanently lost as an export but it was soon supplanted by cotton. Large estates abandoned by Tories during the war in New York, New England, and Pennsylvania were confiscated and divided into small parcels.

At the close of the century, in the first years of nationhood, a New Hampshire historian looked with satisfaction at the small farmers of his time, the citizens Jefferson regarded as the bedrock of democracy. "The people," he wrote, "have the reputation of being good husbandmen, frugal and industrious, and they live much independent."

CHAPTER III
The Farm Worker

THE AMERICAN FARMER has always wanted to "live independent." Unlike his European forebears, he enjoyed the prestige of land ownership. In the Old World, a feudal social system decreed that a man only became a landowner by birth into a landowning class. In the New World, social equality was official doctrine and access to land a basic right. From earliest Colonial days onwards the dominant agricultural pattern has been the owner-operated family farm where all members of the family contribute labor, with little or no assistance from hired help. On the family farm there is no conflict between labor and management, no distinction between those who work in the fields and those who control and administer the property. Those who expend the physical effort required to make the land produce are also those responsible for turning the results of this effort into use and profit. The independence that results from this system is hard won—and highly prized by those who succeed.

The farm laborer, who works for hire, has historically been viewed, not as posing a contradiction to this pattern, but as someone moving up the ladder toward land ownership. In the colonies he was often the young son of a neighboring farmer or the son of the village preacher, blacksmith, or shopkeeper. He enjoyed the same social status as his employer, lived in the farmhouse, and took his meals with the family, sharing their crude diet and participating in family prayers and celebrations. It was expected that he would one day have his own land. Various systems of land tenancy which later evolved have also been seen as rungs toward eventual land ownership, and today it is still commonplace for a young farmer to work as a hired hand, to then rent land from someone else, and still later buy or inherit a farm of his own.

Despite the fact that this satisfying progression has been taking place all across the country all through our history we also know that the agricultural worker *may* be a man or woman totally bereft of any hope of land ownership. Many who have spent a lifetime working on land belonging to others, in a society where this is considered failure, see the relationship between farm owner and farm worker as one of alienation, hostility, and conflict of interest. The problem, of course, did not begin in the twentieth century in the lettuce fields of California. The institution of slavery, which existed for so long in this country, is now regarded by virtually everyone as a national tragedy and disgrace. However, many people remained insensitive to the hopeless plight of the impoverished share-croppers of the post–Civil War period and later, and only recently have most of us been made aware of the ways in which the destitute migratory farm worker has been exploited.

The scarcity of available agricultural laborers in a society that offered free land to all comers was viewed as a problem from early Colonial times. It led to the habit and the glorification of hard work and it also led to cooperative efforts among neighbors so that many tedious time-consuming jobs were accomplished in "bees" and "frolics," where neighbors joined cheerfully in helping each other. It also led to two systems for obtaining unpaid labor: indentured servitude and slavery.

The commonest type of farm laborer in this country in the seventeenth century was not the hired hand but the indentured servant, a bonded white slave. Like the black slave, he worked without wages and his treatment was harsh or relatively humane depending on the inclinations of his master. In the most crucial ways, however, the plight of the indentured servant was very different from that of the African slave since his bondage was usually voluntary and was always of limited duration, whereas that of the black slave was involuntary, life-long, and hereditary.

The white indentured servant was a European, generally from England, Scotland, Ireland, or Germany, who worked a specified limited period of time—commonly three, five, or seven years—to repay his passage from the Old World to the New.

This system originated as a mutually beneficial arrangement in which a person wishing to emigrate who could not pay the cost of transportation or settlement would be provided with passage to the colonies and food and shelter after arrival.

Other indentured servants came involuntarily. Some were kidnapped—many of them vagrants and drunks picked up on the streets of Europe who awakened to find themselves aboard ship. It has been estimated that by 1680 over ten thousand indentured servants had arrived in this country by these illicit means. Convicts—many of them debtors and thieves—were transported to the colonies by the Crown and served indentures. Students of the period think as many as fifty thousand of "His Majesty's seven-year Passengers" were eventually received in this country despite attempts to halt the flow. In all, it is estimated by historians that over half the immigrants to the thirteen colonies settled by the British came as bondsmen.

The westward movement began as land prices in settled areas rose, and a tide of migrants—many of them former indentured servants—moved into unsettled areas in Maryland and Virginia and into the Appalachian Mountains. Some had finished their term of service and some had not. Although he might have been a submissive serf in Europe, in this country, where it was proclaimed that no man was the better of any other, many a bondsman found the idea of being a slave insupportable. If an indentured servant ran away he was unlikely to be caught once he traveled beyond the area where he was known.

Despite the high numbers of agricultural workers under indenture the importation of African slaves began as a response to labor shortages, in the rapidly growing tobacco plantations in the South. As the habit of smoking grew in Europe, large plantations were developed in Virginia and later in Maryland. It is interesting to note that smoking first gained popularity because of its supposed health-giving powers. As early as 1585 an Englishman who went to Virginia as one of the first settlers on the island of Roanoke wrote in his book, *A Briefe and True Report of the New Found Land of Virginia,* "They (the Indians) take the fume or smoke thereofe by sucking it through pipes made of claie into their stomache and heade; from whence it purgeth superflouous fleame and other grosse humors, openth all the pores and passages of the body . . . they know not many greevous diseases wherewithall wee in England are oftentimes afflicted."

As more and more Europeans sought health through smoking, more and more Virginia land was brought under cultivation. One Jamestown settler who had returned to England came back to Virginia in 1617 to find to his astonishment "the market-place, the streets and all other spare places planted with tobacco." That year, the tenth year of settlement, twenty thousand pounds of tobacco were shipped to England. Ten years later the amount exported would climb to five hundred thousand pounds and in 1776 one hundred million pounds would be sent to England from Virginia and Maryland.

King James discouraged the emphasis on one-crop agriculture and directed the Virginians to produce other commodities. The colonists were expected to provide raw materials for which England had grown dependent on foreign lands. Because of reports of the abundant growth of mulberry trees in the colonies, the king urged that a silk industry be established and various unsuccessful attempts were made over the years in a number of southern and some northern colonies. Sheep were sent to the colonies and wool was exported to British mills.

Despite English attempts to restrict tobacco acreage to avoid glutting the market and to assure growing an adequate food supply, the industry expanded rapidly, requiring ever larger crews of agricultural laborers. The number of indentured servants was insufficient, and free men willing to work for wages on plantations were always in short supply. Although there were European intellectuals who were opposed to the view that one person could hold another in bondage, in this country there was little opposition to the importation of Africans as slaves. Slavery had existed since ancient times, and religious authorities pointed out that careful reading of both the Old and New Testaments failed to reveal any injunctions whatsoever against the institution. The inferiority of Africans was, according to most Europeans and colonists, clearly demonstrated both by the color of their skins and by the fact that they were not Christians. Although African slaves were imported by the

Spanish and Portuguese before 1600 to work in their New World colonies, it was not until the end of the seventeenth century that the black slave became the most common type of agricultural laborer on the large plantations of the southern colonies.

Some attempts had been made earlier to enslave Indians, first by the Spanish and Portuguese conquistadores and later by British colonists, particularly in the Carolinas. But the Indians, imbued with their Stone Age culture, were hard to train and, when forced to live closely with whites, demonstrated a lamentable weakness for dying of European diseases to which they had no immunity. The Africans, however, had achieved a sophisticated level of agricultural practice. They had learned in their native lands to grow millet, wheat, rice, cotton, fruits, and vegetables and had owned land individually and collectively and cared for it with great skill. They were accustomed to working in a tropical climate and were experienced not only in raising crops. Many were also able artisans who could fashion knives, saws, and axes from iron, who made pottery, and did weaving and woodworking. Unlike the Indians, they seemed to be of sturdy constitution. Furthermore, it was realistically feared that enslavement of Indians would result in retaliatory massacres whereas the black slave, who could not run off and escape by disappearing into a free native population, was less likely to rebel.

The first slaves to arrive in this country, most of whom went to Virginia, were brought in under a system of limited indenture of four to eight years, and crews of white and black indentured servants worked together in the tobacco fields. As more black laborers arrived and the tide of white laborers slowed, as Europeans learned of the hardships of the new land, the term of service of black workers soon became a lifetime sentence. Laws were enacted which specified that the child of a slave inherited the status of the mother and that birth into slavery was not altered by the race of the father or by receiving Christian baptism.

In the mid-seventeenth century there were only three hundred African laborers in this country, most of them brought in by Dutch slave traders. But with the chartering in England of the Royal Africa Company in the latter part of the century and the enterprises of New World traders, many of whom lived in the northern port cities of Boston, Salem, Providence, New London, and Newport, the sale of human beings became big business and thousands of black slaves were imported annually, some directly from Africa, some from the West Indies.

The cost of a healthy young slave was far beyond the means of most farmers, including most southern landowners, who remained self-sufficient family farmers like most of those in the North. At the time of the outbreak of the Civil War three-quarters of the white families in the South owned no slaves. A small number of slaves had lived with wealthy northern families as household servants, but slavery had existed to a very limited degree in the North and the lack of a commercial agriculture made the institution uneconomical.

All the valuable export crops of the southern plantations required considerable hand labor. It was estimated that one strong slave was needed for the cultivation of three acres of tobacco, a crop that required virtually year-round tending. Prices paid for tobacco in Europe rose quickly, and as the supply of slaves increased, more and more land was brought under cultivation.

Rice growing was particularly unwholesome work and it was widely believed that white laborers could not survive in the swamps, where malaria and yellow fever were commonly contracted. Large quantities of rice were exported to the West Indies, where total concentration on growing sugar led to the necessity for importing all other commodities by the eighteenth century. By the late seventeenth century high quality rice and also indigo were grown in North Carolina, South Carolina, and Georgia, and since both were valuable and also compatible crops they were often grown on the same plantations, leading to more dependence on slaves. Rice grew in low swampy land along the rivers in locations close to the ocean where a system of sluices and ditches made possible periodic flooding of the fields. Indigo required higher, lighter, better drained upland soil. Slaves could work both crops since they required attention at different times of the year.

Indigo gave way to cotton after the Revolutionary War and the invention of the cotton gin in 1793, which solved the

TO BE SOLD, on board the Ship *Bance-Island*, on tuesday the 6th of *May* next, at *Ashley-Ferry*; a choice cargo of about 250 fine healthy **NEGROES**, just arrived from the Windward & Rice Coast. —The utmost care has already been taken, and shall be continued, to keep them free from the least danger of being infected with the SMALL-POX, no boat having been on board, and all other communication with people from *Charles-Town* prevented.

Austin, Laurens, & Appleby.

N. B. Full one Half of the above Negroes have had the SMALL-POX in their own Country.

Slavery Broadside. LIBRARY OF CONGRESS

critical problem of large-scale growing. The success of cotton, which supplanted tobacco as the most important cash crop in the South by 1815, also firmly established the institution of slavery despite the fact that the trans-Atlantic slave trade was officially closed by federal action in 1820 and many thoughtful people, including some influential southerners, had expressed the idea that slavery was inconsistent with the spirit of human equality so stirringly expressed in the new documents of freedom.

But the cotton growers continued exploiting their slaves and their land. As the land became exhausted, growers moved with their slaves to the Black Belt of Alabama, to Mississippi and Louisiana, and by mid-century to Texas. New Orleans and Mobile supplanted Savannah and Charleston as trade centers. Sugar, grown in the bayous of southeastern Louisiana and also in Texas, Florida, and Georgia, was also tended by slaves and productivity grew to outstrip tobacco.

Slave prices were directly influenced by the fluctuating prices received for agricultural staples. Rule of thumb held that if cotton was worth twelve cents a pound a young male slave in good health was worth $1200. During periods of agricultural depression prices fell, and in the mid-1840s a male slave could be purchased for $400. The fifties, however, brought prosperity to southern planters, and the list of a Richmond slave broker in 1852 shows prices ranging from "Best Men" (18 to 25 years) at $1200–1300 down to "Girls four feet tall" at $350 to $450. Later in the decade a sugar planter reported that in New Orleans he had to pay $1,700 for a man, $2,400 for a young woman and her eleven-year-old son, and $2,500 for a slave trained as a blacksmith. Loss of a slave through fatal accident or illness was common and viewed as a financial catastrophe, and this risk, as well as unstable prices, unfavorable weather, and uncontrollable insect invasion, kept many planters deeply in debt. By 1860 the southern slave population was about four million, having grown rapidly through natural increase and illegal trade from one million in 1810.

At the end of the Civil War agriculture in the South was at a standstill as landowners found themselves with devastated land, without money, and without credit. All stored food sup-

Slave family on J. J. Smith plantation, Beaufort, South Carolina, 1862. LIBRARY OF CONGRESS

plies had been taken or destroyed by Federal armies. The former slaves, who had been led to expect that the Federal Government would seize the plantations and divide them into forty-acre farms to be given to the new freedmen, found their hopes blasted. It soon became clear that Reconstruction leaders in Congress were offering neither land, nor equipment and training to help them start new lives. The moral impetus that drove Northerners during the war quickly died down and the black family was on its own.

In 1865, 1866, and 1867 crop failures due to drought led to ruin for both white and black farmers and many blacks left the still totally agricultural South to seek jobs in northern industrial cities. An adventurous few went west, despite the fact that they were excluded from receiving free land under the provisions of the Homestead Act. Many were turned off the plantations and wandered the South looking for work. It was estimated that during the winter of 1865, seventy thousand blacks in eastern Virginia had become homeless. Although a large number of former slaves had been given land after emancipation by former masters, most of these holdings were lost due to lack of capital, inexperience, bad management, and the total absence of black lawyers, bankers, or other trained advisors who might have been able to help. By 1900 black farmers in Georgia had title to only 4 percent of the land, although they constituted half the state's population.

Many of the former slaves remained at the old plantations. At first a wage system was instituted, but because a huge new post-war class of indigent white farm workers would not labor in the fields with blacks, a new form of quasi-slavery was established for both poor black and poor white farmers known as the sharecropper system. The landowner divided his total acreage into small parcels with a small shack erected on each. Each sharecropper and his family lived on their section, paying the owner for land rent and provisions with a share of the crop. Although he was not a slave, the sharecropper soon found himself locked in the cycle of poverty, ignorance, and dependence. The white sharecropper did no better than the black in breaking out of the cycle, despite the fact that most had once owned and managed their own farms and were at first thought of as temporarily landless. By the end of the nineteenth century white sharecroppers outnumbered black sharecroppers on the cotton and tobacco farms of the South.

Farm tenancy in the South as it began after the Civil War and continued through the 1930s took three forms. The "cash tenant" owned farm implements and draft animals and had enough money to buy seed and fertilizer and sustain his family while waiting for the harvest. He rented the land from the owner, paid cash, and tried to save enough money to buy his own farm. The "share tenant" was much more common and his economic position was considerably less secure. He owned some tools and work animals but needed the landlord's help in buying supplies. The landlord also extended credit to the share tenant family to maintain them during the long growing season. After the harvest, the landowner received a percentage of the crop—usually one quarter to one third—in payment.

The third kind of farm tenant was the sharecropper or "cropper." He was the poorest of the tenants in the South. He and his wife and children had nothing to offer except their labor. The landlord supplied acreage, a house, animals, seed, fertilizer, and provisions through credit at the plantation store and received half the crop in rent. Settlement time came when the sharecropper's cotton was sold and the landlord deducted from the cropper's half a sum equivalent to the money he had advanced for food and all other goods as well as fees for management. Some landowners kept honest records; others took full advantage of the cropper's ignorance of bookkeeping. Although sharecropper families waited all year for the money they hoped to realize at settlement time, most often they found themselves as desperately needy then as they had been before.

The sharecropper system persisted in the South until World War II brought an end to the Great Depression and large numbers of poor southern farmers left rural areas for jobs in defense plants. As the sharecropper system died out, the demand for cheap agricultural labor persisted. Many of the remaining poor black farmers became migrant workers who traveled from South to North each year as crops grew ready for harvesting, starting in the winter in Florida and moving north through the Carolinas, the Middle Atlantic states, New York,

Migrant laborers picking snap beans in New York State, 1967. UNITED STATES DEPARTMENT OF AGRICULTURE *(following page)*

and even to Maine during the spring and summer months.

Before the breakup of the sharecropper system resulted in a supply of migrant black farm workers, East Coast farmers had relied on recently arrived white immigrants for help at harvest time. In vegetable fields and cranberry bogs, in orchards and on berry farms, Italians, Portuguese, Polish, and other settlers in New Jersey, New York, and Massachusetts worked the harvests in their areas. Very young children formed a high percentage of the labor crews.

West Coast farmers had employed migrant workers as early as the 1870s. The first seasonal farm workers, who were employed on the fruit and vegetable farms in California, were Chinese men originally brought over to work on building the intercontinental railroad. They were followed in the 1890s by Japanese, and in this century by Filipinos, Mexicans, and in the 1930s by refugees from the "dust bowls" of Oklahoma, Arkansas, and Texas.

In 1976 a U.S. Department of Agriculture study found that the average annual farm-worker income was $1,652 and that half of these seasonal workers had no other form of employment. The National Labor Relations Act of 1935, which established collective bargaining procedures for industrial workers and is considered the Magna Carta of organized labor, was strongly opposed by Southern agricultural interests, and to avoid defeat of the bill, Congress specifically excluded agricultural workers from coverage. Until recent years farm workers were also uniformly excluded from child labor laws, Social Security, minimum wage laws, unemployment insurance programs, and workmen's compensation acts. Some changes are taking place in several states but Department of Labor inspectors have found children working illegally on 60 percent of farms, and the American Friends Service Committee estimates the number of child pickers at eight hundred thousand, at great detriment to their schooling and health.

When a labor shortage occurred during the early period of the Korean War, 1950 to 1951, growers put pressure on Congressmen, and Public Law 78—known as the "bracero program" —permitted the entry of three hundred thousand Mexican laborers annually, who were willing to work for the lowest

After a day working in lettuce fields, Mexican farm workers are bussed back to the Mexican border, 1975. UNITED STATES DEPARTMENT OF AGRICULTURE

wages. The "temporary" program was in effect from 1951 until 1964 despite objections from Mexican-American farm workers, and thousands still enter, some illegally and some with official work visas. Growers have always preferred non-English speaking laborers, who are difficult to unionize. Because of an oversupply of cheap labor, strikes have historically been ineffective.

Attention was focused on the problem when Cesar Chavez, a Mexican-American who grew up on his family's farm in Arizona, was successful in organizing the United Farm Workers of America in 1966. A gifted leader and a magnetic and spiritual man, he preached nonviolence in a struggle rife with violence. Through strikes, fasts, and boycott appeals to sympathetic consumers, he attracted the concern of politicians, religious leaders, and investigative reporters to "la causa," and in 1970 many large producers signed labor contracts giving pickers higher wages, committing growers to contribute to medical plans and to regulate the use of dangerous pesticides. But farm workers still receive a minimum wage below that of industrial workers. Although farming is considered the third most dangerous occupation—following mining and construction—most states do not have workmen's compensation provisions. California, in 1975, was the first state to enact an agricultural labor relations act.

In 1951 a Presidential Commission on Migratory Labor reported that "migrants are the children of misfortune. We depend on misfortune to build up our force of migratory workers and when the supply is low because there is not enough misfortune at home, we rely on misfortune abroad to replenish the supply." Three decades later the widespread exploitation of the farm worker continues to bring shame on the wealthiest nation on earth.

Migratory farm families across the country show shockingly high incidences of vitamin deficiency diseases, and other illnesses related to poor living standards. Life expectancy is twenty years under the national average and infant mortality rates are three times higher. Only recently have figures on thousands of incidents of severe pesticide poisoning among farm workers been gathered, and growers still battle regulations prohibiting premature re-entry into sprayed fields.

CHAPTER IV
The Public Domain

ALTHOUGH SYSTEMS OF LAND DISTRIBUTION have varied throughout our history, the official guiding philosophy from Revolutionary times until the closing of the frontier in the late nineteenth century was the Jeffersonian ideal that as many Americans as possible should become landowners. In the Colonial period, similar convictions guided land distribution practices and lured landless Europeans to brave the hardships of the New World. Officially, this philosophy opposed the amassing of large tracts by individual farmers, "gentleman" farmers, and land speculators. Abuses of both public policy and specific legislation have been rampant in all periods and yet it was possible, during a span of almost three centuries, for any white man who wanted to farm and was willing to move into a frontier area to acquire land free or at very little cost.

In the seventeenth century, immigrants to the colonies received grants of land without cost under systems that varied from one colony to another. In Virginia fifty-acre parcels were offered by the Crown as a "headright" to each settler. Fifty additional acres were also granted for each person the settler brought to America, including family members and household servants. This system was later adopted in Maryland and the Carolinas where one hundred fifty rather than fifty acres were granted each settler and in Georgia where as many as five hundred acres were given to those who would bring over ten indentured servants. These servants often became entitled to headrights of their own after completing their term of labor.

In the northern colonies land was distributed in smaller parcels on the basis of family size and other considerations, which often were political, and a typical farm consisted of twelve to twenty acres. The seventeenth century New England family farm was not the self-contained piece of fenced-in land with house and barn that most of us imagine. People erected their dwellings on small plots located close together for security and access to the Common where livestock could graze. In this way, towns grew. Each family also owned several parcels of meadow and perhaps some marshland, where the wild salt hay could be cut for use as animal feed. A farmer might also be granted some acreage far from his dwelling, with parcels of the best and the least desirable land in the area distributed by lot. Each family had pasturage rights in the Common—a large central grassy area dedicated as a common field where citizens could stroll, the militia could drill, and animals graze. Livestock kept on the Common were tended by town shepherds. The size of a man's holding determined the number and type of farm animals he could pasture.

The "town system" of New England and the "headright system" of the southern colonies resulted in a reasonably equitable distribution of land although some vast estates and plantations were established as early as the seventeenth century, particularly by friends of the King and by other wealthy settlers in Virginia, Pennsylvania, and Maryland and in the colony of New York after British takeover from the Dutch. The tobacco-growing southern plantations often exceeded five thousand acres, with slaves doing all the field labor, household work, carpentry, milling, shoemaking, weaving, and spinning.

Land speculation began early in the eighteenth century when both the town system and the headright system collapsed as local governments sold fields and common lands to raise money to pay debts, erect public schools, town halls, and libraries. Although the primitive tools and methods of the first half of the seventeenth century made farming even a few acres heavy work, pressures for larger farms increased as plows became more common and it was feasible to cultivate large acreage.

As free land became unavailable in well-settled areas, those without the means to purchase farms from landholders or from the Crown moved west over the Alleghenies, beginning a tradition of mobility that still typifies the American. King George, fearful of inciting further Indian wars, ordered their return, indicating that farmers were not to move beyond a line of settlement at the crest of the mountains: "We do strictly forbid, on pain of our displeasure, all our loving subjects from making any purchases or settlements whatever in that region." Although some attempt was made to halt the migration, the result of the edict was simply to increase resentment against British rule.

Settlements were also made before the Revolution in the Mississippi Valley, where pioneers who were prepared to battle wilderness, isolation, and Indians found good access to markets along the Ohio and Mississippi rivers and their tributaries. Others went to what is now West Virginia and from southwestern Virginia through the Cumberland Gap to Kentucky. By 1761 Daniel Boone and other hunters had visited Tennessee.

The policy of offering land bounties to war veterans, both as reward for service and as incentive to encourage enlistment, began in 1646 and continued into the nineteenth century. In 1776 the Congress offered grants of land to Hessians employed by the British if they would desert the military, and at the end of the war it was estimated that one out of five of these twenty thousand Hessian mercenaries had accepted the offer.

The difficulties and deprivations involved in moving into a frontier wilderness and converting it to farmland quickly defeated many courageous adventurers. Others struggled against drought, insect invasion, and the pain of isolation for years on land they were finally forced to abandon. But thousands succeeded as the American frontier moved from the Atlantic coast slowly westward. To the restless American farmer the idea of opportunity became synonymous with this steady movement into new lands, and the sacrifices made by all family members to realize the dream led to a fierce independence of character that has been celebrated in countless stories, dramas, and films.

The necessity for specific laws that would permit transfer of western lands to individuals as the population grew and spread, starting in 1796, resulted in a series of land acts that

Homesteader family plowing. UNITED STATES DEPARTMENT OF AGRICULTURE

culminated in the Homestead Act of 1862. The acts varied in the amount of land offered, the price per acre, and the terms of payment. At first land was offered in parcels of 640 acres at a dollar an acre, requiring the outlay of a sum of money very few farmers could afford. Wealthy speculators rushed in to buy land from the government which they then divided and resold in small parcels to settlers. Demands for smaller offerings of land led to more liberal policies. The demand for land in the West continued to grow, due to increasingly high land prices in the East, the rise in population, and the wasteful land practices that had destroyed the fertility of the soil in many older areas. The population in the colonies in 1690 was approximately two hundred thousand. By 1790, at the time of the first census, 94 percent of the then four million Americans were living in the thirteen original states and most of the rest in Ohio, Kentucky, and Tennessee. By 1850, there were twenty-three million Americans living in thirty-one states.

Eastern landowners opposed liberal public land policies which, they felt, would damage the market for farmland in the East and encourage migration, but the movement to the new lands never abated. Territories were opened up by explorers, who were followed by Indian traders and hunters, and later by armies of settlers seeking fertile land in desirable locations.

In 1845 over five thousand bold adventurers made the trip west when gold was discovered in California and many settled there and farmed. By 1856 California farmers were exporting grain and flour to Peru, and two lines of settlement had been established with some pioneers moving eastward from California into unexplored areas and others traveling west from the Mississippi River across the great plains.

In advance of the line of settlement there was inevitably land grabbing by individuals and corporations, which amassed, by fair means and foul, by purchase and by political clout, much of the most desirable land. Large areas of the best timber and mining land went to large corporations. Congress and state legislators authorized the granting of huge areas of prime farmland as an inducement to the railroads, in the belief that the government should help capitalists finance necessary public

54

Homesteader family in Wisconsin. UNITED STATES DEPARTMENT OF AGRICULTURE

improvements. Some of this land was used for new rail routes; some was sold at very high rates when proposed lines failed to be constructed. Accessibility to transportation was always highly desirable and farmers paid extortionist prices for land near new lines that the railroads had received free.

As early as 1844 free soil advocates such as George Henry Evans were proposing "equal rights to every man to the free use of a sufficient portion of the Earth to till for his subsistence." The western farmer, who coped with attempting to make arid land productive, had become crippled by debt and felt himself the victim of land grabbers and eastern bankers. There was increased demand that the government make lands available for farming by people who could not afford to pay for it.

The result was the Homestead Act of 1862, which stated that any American citizen or immigrant alien who was twenty-one years old or the head of a family or had served fourteen days in military service could, by paying a ten-dollar fee to file a claim, acquire one hundred sixty acres of unsettled public land. After living on it and cultivating it for five years he would receive final title. If he wished he had the option of residing on the land for only six months, paying $1.25 an acre, and receiving title. Abraham Lincoln, in signing the act, said, "I am in favor of settling the wild lands into small parcels so that every poor man may have a home."

The railroads, which opened land in new frontier areas, needed settlements along their routes as a source of freight revenue, and they sent pamphlets to European countries, in their native languages, urging people to come to the new territories. Agents hawked the availability of free homesteads in European cities and at ports. One circular from the Northern Pacific Railroad assured Scandinavians that the only threat to health in the state of Montana was overeating. To people who had heard about lack of rainfall in the West the railroads sent assurances that "rain follows the plow."

The settlers came. Eastern farmers headed west and new waves of immigration from Europe followed earlier waves. German immigrants had started coming in large numbers before 1840, settling the lake region near Milwaukee. Earlier

56

still, German immigrants had settled in Pennsylvania where, in 1789, Benjamin Rush noted "the superior size of their barns, the height of their enclosures, the extent of their orchards, the fertility of their fields, the luxuriance of their meadows, and the general appearance of plenty and neatness in everything that belongs to them." Although most of the Italian and Polish immigrants went to the towns, Scandinavians came in large numbers from 1850 to 1880 and settled in the upper Midwest, where they found the climate familiar. Bohemians, Russians, Irish, Welsh, and English newcomers, along with Swiss and Finns, settled on farms in the Midwest and the Prairie States. Large numbers of German-Russians, who had migrated to the Ukraine to escape persecution in the eighteenth century, moved on to America in the nineteenth when persecutions began in Russia, and found employment in the sugar beet fields of Colorado.

The pioneers settled along the muddy Missouri River, which Senator Thomas Hart Benton described as too thick to swim in and too thin to walk on. They went to western Missouri, Iowa, eastern Kansas, and Nebraska. In Nebraska and Kansas they built rough sod houses and burned dried "cow chips" for fuel in the woodless prairie and, until the invention of barbed wire, planted thorn hedges to enclose their pastures.

In the 1870s a trickle of emancipated black families headed for the frontier, an estimated twenty thousand by 1880. A large group settled in Graham County, Kansas, establishing a town they named Nicodemus. Because of lack of horses and equipment the farmers and their wives and children worked, as the first settlers did, with only hoes and mattocks. The town later had a band, an academy, and a Masonic Lodge, and a farmer's son from Nicodemus was sent to the capital as state auditor.

The settlers on the prairies and the Great Plains suffered drought, hot summer winds that damaged the crops, autumn prairie fires, blizzards and sub-zero weather in winter. They suffered insect invasions such as "the grasshopper year" of 1878, which ravaged the Dakotas, Nebraska, Kansas, and parts of Texas and Missouri. The grasshoppers, which came suddenly on a late July day, arrived in such numbers that they made a sound like hail on the roofs, consumed all the crops and the

A band of Russian immigrants passing through South Dakota, 1894.
SOUTH DAKOTA STATE HISTORICAL SOCIETY *(following page)*

leaves on the trees, lay so thickly on the tracks that they stopped the trains of the Union Pacific. One covered wagon heading east with a discouraged farm family bore a sign saying, "From Sodom, where it rains grasshoppers, fire and destruction." At all times pioneers in covered wagons heading west met others returning eastward. One family noted a sign on a deserted cabin in a drought area of Texas that read: "250 miles to the nearest post office, 100 miles to wood, 20 miles to water, 6 inches to Hell. God bless our home. Gone to live with wife's folks."

The Homestead Act, which seemed the culmination of the free soil advocates' dream, has been widely criticized. Although the intent of the Act was to settle the hinterland, reduce the federal land monopoly, and also provide land for needy people from the crowded East, the cost of transportation to the free lands in the West, of buying equipment and animals, of survival until the first crops were available was an impossible sum for the impoverished eastern farmer or urban laborer. There were no provisions for bringing poor families to the farms or for offering them credit or guidance. By the time the Act took effect, a high percentage of the remaining land was semi-arid. Speculation in western lands continued, since cash sale was not eliminated until 1891, and much of the richest land left in the public domain continued to be bought directly from the government by timber dealers, cattle grazers, mining corporations, and land speculators. Would-be homesteaders were often forced to buy land instead of claiming it, in order to acquire fertile acreage with access to transportation, schools, and other necessities.

During all these years Congress continued giving free land to the railroads to encourage continuation of construction, with the provision that if the railroad was not built over this land it was to be sold to settlers at $1.25 an acre or returned to the government. This law, however, was not enforced and such parcels went at high prices. It is estimated that genuine homesteaders received only about one in six of the eighty million acres given away by the government between 1860 and 1900, with the rest going to investors who often established mock "settlements" in the form of portable cabins or tents with boards tacked to one side, to the railroads, to states for canals and wagon roads. Absentee owners pieced together huge properties of thousands of acres in the Red River Valley area of North Dakota and Minnesota where, a century ahead of our industrialized modern farms, they grew spectacular harvests of wheat on "bonanza farms," using professional management, specialized horse-drawn equipment, and at harvest time, battalions of laborers from Chicago and other midwestern cities.

The Homestead Act has also been criticized for failure to recognize that, in the semi-arid areas, grazing was more suitable than crop growing, and cattle ranchers needed considerably more than 160 acres for a profitable operation. New "dry farming" methods, in which half the land was left fallow each year to accumulate moisture so that only half a crop could be grown, also required greater acreage. Thousands of those who attempted to raise crops in the Central Plains areas of western Kansas, Nebraska, and the eastern regions of Colorado left at the end of the 1880s, threatened by starvation after a long series of dry years. Some crossed to the Pacific Coast, claiming agricultural land in high rainfall areas in Oregon and Washington.

As desirable land disappeared, farmers began covetously viewing lands guaranteed to the Indians. The availability of a public domain for distribution to citizens had resulted from large land purchases and confinement of the Indians to reservations through literally hundreds of treaties, which were written between 1774 and 1871. By 1870, 138 million acres of public lands had been assigned to the Indians living west of the Mississippi and Missouri rivers "for as long as the grass shall grow and the rivers shall run," in the traditional treaty terms. But in 1870 the governor of the Colorado Territory complained of the fact that "these indolent savages" were occupying "the best portion of my territory." The gift of lands to the Indians evolved into "Indian giving," as acreage not actually occupied by the tribal people was, bit by bit, opened to settlement by farmers, with the Indians offered food and clothing or transfer to territory in Oklahoma in exchange.

In 1889 the Cherokee strip in Oklahoma was open to settlement. Since the number of homesteaders far exceeded the number of available homesteads, the device of the land rush was established. At noon on April 22, 1889, soldiers fired pistols, and horsemen, men in buggies and wagons, runners, and even men on bicycles raced through "a great cloud of dust hovering like smoke over a battlefield," in the words of one participant, to stake their claims. By afternoon, plows were breaking the soil. The "boomers," so-called, took the law into their own hands when they found settlers, whom they called "sooners," who had sneaked into the territory ahead of schedule in the dark of night to stake claims. One man was found shot, with a note pinned to his shirt, saying simply, TOO SOON. One participant wrote, "a country two hours old with a boomer sitting on every square half mile—or perhaps even three or four gentlemen sitting on the same quarter section and regarding each other with disfavor—still looks remarkably like untouched prairie."

In the 1890s, invasions were made into one Indian reservation after another. Although Federal lands were not withdrawn from settlement until 1935, with some reopening of homesteading in 1946, most of the land remaining by the end of the nineteenth century was suitable only for grazing or for forest or wildlife preserves. The American farmer had entered a new period in history. The frontier had vanished. It was no longer possible to leave ill fortune and error behind and push west into new land.

CHAPTER V

The Start of the Modern Era

ALL THROUGH THE NINETEENTH CENTURY, as the line of settlement advanced, eastern farm family life, compared with that of the pioneer farmer in the West, was safe, cozy, social, companionable. Nathaniel Hawthorne, on a trip through the Massachusetts countryside in 1841, "saw no absolutely mean or poor looking abodes. They were warm and comfortable farmhouses." Visitors to New England from other countries commented on the charm of the early saltbox homes built of clapboard, painted white, with fresh green shutters.

Life was becoming more luxurious even in a recently settled area of South Carolina where, half in sorrow, half in pride, a farmer told his tale in an article titled "Cause of Hard Times," in an early issue of *The Southern Agriculturist*. The farmer, father of many daughters, boasted that he had, through his frugality, managed to save 150 silver dollars: "My farm gave me and my whole family a good living on the produce of it . . . for I never spent more than $10 a year, which was for salt and nails and the like. Nothing to wear, eat or drink was purchased as my farm provided all." One day, however, when his third daughter was to be married his wife, as he wrote, "comes for the purse; but when she returned, what did I see! A silken gown, silk for a cloak, a looking glass . . ." and a china tea set and other luxuries and "an empty purse." And this was not the end of the spending. By the time his last daughter was married, he reported, the once bare house contained "all sorts of household furniture unknown to us before" and his harvest of flax and the wool of his sheep was being sold to buy ribbons and silk, tea and sugar.

For the farmer in the West life was not silk and ribbons and even salt and nails were hard to come by. In 1835, in his *Democracy in America,* the French observer Alexis de Tocqueville described this scene. On entering a one-room log dwelling, he saw, "In the center of the room a rude table, with legs of green wood with the bark still on them, looking as if they grew out of the ground on which they stood." On the rough mantle were a Bible, a book of Shakespeare's plays and Milton's poems.

Pioneers in Kansas described their new home in a song:

> Oh, the hinges are of leather,
> And the windows have no glass
> While the roof it lets the howling blizzard in;
> And you can hear the hungry coyote
> As he sneaks up through the grass
> In that little old sod shanty on the claim.

At the time materials for a sod house cost three dollars including a window, a stovepipe, and a latch for the door. Since a frame house cost two hundred and fifty dollars, most people chose to build out of sod. In summer a sod house turned from brown to green as grass sprouted from the walls.

In the new territories farm families were reliving the hardships faced by the first settlers, while in the East farmers were enjoying such educational and recreational innovations as the new agricultural journals and the festive country fairs.

Interest in scientific agriculture predated the nineteenth century, but in the early years was confined to elite societies of learned men, none of whom depended on farming for a living. The Philadelphia Society for Promoting Agriculture was founded in 1785 with a membership composed of George Washington, four signers of the Constitution, and many Revolutionary War officers. Publications of the society centered on land use, new seed varieties, animal husbandry, and suggestions for elimination of the wheat pest known as Hessian fly, thought to have been brought into the country in the straw bedding of Hessian mercenary soldiers during the Revolution.

Soon other agricultural societies were formed. The Columbian Agricultural Society was established in Washington,

64

Homesteaders in front of sod dugout adjoining shed, Nebraska, c. 1890. UNITED STATES DEPARTMENT OF AGRICULTURE

D.C. in 1809. The Berkshire Agricultural Society of Western Massachusetts sponsored the first agricultural fair in 1811. In the 1820s state legislatures were induced to offer financial aid for the societies and the educational fairs they were more and more commonly promoting. By 1820 there were agricultural societies in virtually all counties in the New England states, and the fairs they sponsored, at which awards from state funds were offered for the biggest, best-looking crops and the heaviest animals, were the highlights of the farm family's year.

With literacy rates rising, journals dedicated to informing and entertaining farm families became popular. *The American Farmer,* started in 1819 in Calvert County, Maryland, was followed quickly by *The Ploughboy* in Albany, New York. Soon afterwards *The New England Farmer, The New York Farmer, The Southern Agriculturist* and others entered the competition. All idealized the life of the farmer as opposed to that of his city cousin. An article in *The New England Farmer* directed toward young readers warns against the "drinking, gaming, and other low, vulgar, and degrading associations and amusements so called," which city people enjoy. It advised young men to choose farming as a profession, stressing "how much more useful and honorable" it is to seek "the invigorating toils of the field and the never tiring studies of nature, renouncing the unmanly and enervating pleasures and pursuits of the town."

By 1850 there were forty thriving magazines filled with hints on new ways of preserving parsnips, making starch from wheat, spinning silk, making corn pudding and cider bread, brewing home remedies for eye inflammations and burns. They included, in a typical issue, suggestions on feed for horses and oxen, notes on beekeeping, advice for using vegetable matter to improve soils—"those which produce the most putrid and nauseous effluvia during fermentation were found producing the most active effect on the growing crop." Challenged by rising urbanization the journals warned young people who were needed on the farm about the horrors of the city with an ever-increasing urgency. City folk, they said, were doomed to "lives of dissipation, of reckless speculation, of ultimate crime."

Despite such warnings, children of northeastern farmers were

County Fair. SMITHSONIAN INSTITUTION

lured to the large urban centers that resulted from industrial development. These centers also brought about a greatly expanded domestic market for farm commodities. Whereas the typical subsistence farmer of 1800 grew food for his family with a small surplus for sale or barter, the farmer of the mid-nineteenth century found that he could sell fresh vegetables, fruits, milk, butter, cheese, and other perishables to city people, and with the money he earned he could buy the manufactured products for which he had developed a taste: cloth, tools, shoes, tableware, furniture, candles, soap—all formerly made at home. The farmer, who had previously raised crops on the basis of family needs, became a businessman who grew crops for sale, making decisions about fruit and vegetable varieties and livestock on the basis of market demand.

Specialization began as large fruit orchards were developed in New York State and potato growing became centered in Maine and on Long Island. Farmers growing a diversity of crops still predominated in all areas of the country, but they were going against current trends and the advice offered in their agricultural journals.

Wheat and corn continued to be grown for domestic consumption in the East but large-scale production of both commodities had moved west. Corn production moved from Kentucky, Tennessee, and Virginia to Illinois, Ohio, Missouri, Indiana, Iowa, Kansas, and Nebraska. Wheat production became established in Ohio, Indiana, Michigan, Illinois, and Wisconsin, where yields were four times those in the East. Journalist Hamlin Garland recalled his childhood on an Iowa farm in the 1860s in his *A Son of the Middle Border.*

> We were all worshippers of wheat in those days. The men thought and talked of little else between seeding and harvest, and you will not wonder at this if you have known and bowed before such abundance as we then enjoyed . . . We trembled when the storm lay hard upon the wheat, we exulted as the lilac shadows of noonday drifted over it . . . We stood before it at evening when the setting sun flooded it with crimson, the bearded heads lazily swirling under the wings of the wind . . .

and our hearts expanded with the beauty and mystery of it—and back of all this was the knowledge that its abundance meant a new carriage, an addition to the house, or a new suit of clothes.

The development of large growing areas in the West that fed dense populations in the East and in Europe was made possible by advances in transportation. In the early years produce traveled east by the Cumberland Road, but in much greater quantity through the Great Lakes and the Erie Canal, which opened in 1825. Hogs and corn proved to be a profitable combination. At first hogs were driven cross-country on foot, as professional drovers led herds as large as five thousand eastward at the rate of eight to ten miles a day. Later, as the railroads expanded, meat-packing centers were established and Cincinnati became known as "Porkopolis." Since beef was harder to preserve without refrigeration than pork, cattle drives to the East continued long after the hog drives stopped.

In the East, commercial canneries were opened in Massachusetts, Maine, New York, Maryland, and Delaware in the mid-nineteenth century, and some farmers began selling fruits and vegetables to food processors as well as directly to consumers. Heat processing of foods had begun early in the century as farm families learned the new method of preserving fruits and vegetables at harvest time by cooking the food after it was packed in hermetically sealed jars, a method first developed in France. Suddenly the pleasures of summer came to the table in winter, whereas previously only meats and grains had been available. When the manufacture of tin plated steel cans began in 1847, the new canned goods became available in country and city stores stacked next to the gunnysacks of potatoes, grains, and nuts, the barrels of crackers and whale oil and bags of beans and coffee. Soon after 1860 virtually anything that could be cooked was being commercially canned and the canning process became fully automated well before the end of the century. These first "convenience foods" altered the eating habits of the nation, overturning the concept of seasonability in diet. Although commercial canning began on a small scale, concurrent developments in transportation and the swelling of the population by the arrival of hundreds of thousands of new immigrants gave impetus to the growth of the industry. Some canners had teams of salesmen who rode into town by stagecoach or train, visiting rural stores on horseback and selling large and small storekeepers on the high quality of the new canned goods.

It was the railroad that tied the grower, processor, wholesaler, and retailer into the closely knit chain we call the food distribution industry, which now handles, processes, and packages nearly 150 million tons of products in a year. In 1830 only twenty-three miles of track had been laid but by 1840 there were two thousand. In 1860 the railroad lines had expanded to thirty thousand miles and in 1869 the ceremonial driving of the golden spike marked completion of the first transcontinental line, joining eastern and western branches. That same year the first carload of bananas was carried by train from California to New York. Railroad track gauges were standardized going north and south along the East Coast, so cargoes could be hauled long distances without being loaded and unloaded from one line to another, and perishable crops could be carried from moderate southeastern climes to chilly northern industrial centers. Large citrus groves were established along the Indian River on Florida's Atlantic Coast and the St. John's River on the Gulf Coast as well as in Texas and Arizona. Standardization of railroad gauges further west made possible the shipment of cattle for a thousand or more miles from Texas ranches to the city of Chicago, which became the meat packing center of the country in the 1860s.

The need to transport meat and fresh produce and have it arrive at its destination in good condition brought about the development of the refrigerated railroad car and the establishment of vast year-round growing areas in parts of California, New Mexico, Texas, and Florida, far from the densely populated cities. Strawberries arrived in New York in winter packed among blocks of ice on sawdust-covered floors of the new cars. Spoilage rates were high and prices charged made such luxuries available only to the very rich. The first "modern" refrigerator cars were built in 1880, with improved insulation and special metal compartments that held the ice, and were refilled at

Men with scythes. UNITED STATES DEPARTMENT OF AGRICULTURE

"Combined harvester," now known as the combine, c. 1900. UNITED
STATES DEPARTMENT OF AGRICULTURE *(following page)*

stops along the route east. It was not until 1950 that these cars were replaced by mechanically cooled rail cars with diesel engines powering generators to electrify the refrigeration equipment.

In New England and the Middle-Atlantic States colonial methods of farming remained virtually unchanged until the middle of the nineteenth century. Tools were primitive and clumsy, with oxen the chief draft animals, and most plows were homemade wooden contrivances with some iron parts fashioned by the local blacksmith. With an increased market for his production, however, the farmer looked for better tools and began replacing the slow moving oxen with the more agile horse.

The western farmer had found that the old fashioned plows worked poorly on the thick, sticky sod. A steel plow invented in 1837 by John Deere, an Illinois blacksmith, proved workable, and the high polish kept the heavy sod from sticking to the moldboard.

The steel plow was one of a number of new inventions for increasing agricultural production. In 1834 Cyrus McCormick invented a mechanical horse-drawn reaper that replaced manpower at the point in production of grain when delay in reaping could mean loss of the harvest. The farmer was still limited to growing only as much as he could reap before it became overripe, but now he could reap more efficiently and greatly increase his acreage and productivity. A variety of mechanical planters, grain drills, and cultivators were patented, and later in the century the combine, which cut, threshed, cleaned, and bagged grain in a single operation was invented, combining the jobs previously accomplished by two machines, the reaper and the thresher. The first combines were enormous mechanisms pulled by teams of as many as forty horses or mules. The largest, most expensive pieces of farm equipment were owned by teams of men who made the circuit from farm to farm at harvest time. Northern farmers in the East were more conservative than the western wheat and corn growers. They became interested in the new machinery only when faced by lack of

Steam-powered tractor. SMITHSONIAN INSTITUTION

manpower and high prices offered for farm produce during the Civil War.

As dependence on expensive horse-powered and later steam-powered equipment became more common, and as production increased proportionally and the farm journals continued to urge specialization, the American farmer moved farther and farther from a life of simple self-sufficiency. He became vitally interested in and dependent on fluctuations in demand and in price. He was immersed in buying and selling, in making payments and in keeping a safe margin of profit. He was aware of himself as a businessman in competition with bigger businessmen, in debt to the bank for his land and his equipment. He might even have mortgaged his farm to buy equipment. Many farmers were beginning to use the new expensive commercial fertilizers in an attempt to further increase production. Peruvian guano was first imported for this purpose in 1843, and by 1860 there were seven American factories producing fertilizers that farmers purchased while tossing barn manure out into the road. The time required to produce one acre of wheat had been reduced from seventy-five hours in 1830 to thirteen hours in 1880 and during the second half of the nineteenth century wheat yields went up seven times while corn yields increased four and a half times.

The first farm organization that made its influence felt politically was the Patrons of Husbandry, more popularly known as the Grange. It was founded in 1867 in Washington, D.C. and spread to every section of the country, finding particular support in the Midwest. In New England, where there was less mortgage indebtedness and where farmers were closer to market, there was less initial support. Started by Oliver Kelly, a Department of Agriculture employee who was concerned about the social and economic deprivations of small farmers, it was originally conceived as a social and educational order with secret rites similar to those of Freemasonry. But once the farmers were brought together—in 15,000 local branches with one and one half million members by 1874—political groups were formed. As Grange suppers, debates, picnics continued to bring recreation to country people, slates of candidates for political

THE FARMERS' MOVEMENT IN THE WEST.—MEETING OF THE GRANGERS IN THE WOODS NEAR WINCHESTER, SCOTT COUNTY, ILLINOIS.—Sketched by Jos. B. Beale.—See Page 335.

Meeting of the Grangers in the woods near Winchester, Scott County, Illinois, sketched by Jos. B. Beale, 1873. LIBRARY OF CONGRESS

office who were sympathetic to the concerns of farmers were drawn up and elected in predominantly rural states. They had some success in regulating railroad freight rates, an issue of great concern in the Midwest and the West.

Increased production with the new machinery and competition from other countries had led to alarming price drops. Between 1867 and 1868 corn went from 57 cents to 32 cents a bushel and wheat from $1.45 to 78 cents. To the farmer heavily in debt for his equipment such low prices spelled ruin. He blamed the railroad for high freight rates and the bankers who foreclosed on loans and the middlemen for high prices on necessary farm supplies and equipment.

The farm community, which had accounted for 90 percent of the population of the country in the early years of the nineteenth century, had dropped radically as young people migrated to the cities. In 1886 farmers made up only 43 percent of the total labor force. But in most states the voters were still predominantly employed in agriculture. The Grange became a major force in elevating the new Department of Agriculture, formed by the Federal government in 1862, to cabinet status, in having agriculture taught in the public schools, and, by 1896, in the achievement of rural mail delivery.

Many Grange objectives failed but the organization proved that farmers could work together, despite their prized individualism, to advance their own interests. Membership in the Grange peaked in 1875 and began to wane as new organizations, which had started up in the 1870s, particularly the Farmers' Alliances, began to ascend, establishing grain elevators in Minnesota and the Dakotas, cooperative creameries in Illinois, cooperative cotton gins and grain elevators in the South and cooperative cotton marketing. The Alliances tackled the problem of horse thievery, offered insurance and credit, and extended cooperative buying and selling. Unfortunately, many of the substantial discounts they offered on farm implements were available only to those who could pay cash. The Colored Farmer's National Alliance and Cooperative Union, which had been established in 1886 in Texas, had grown to a membership of one and one-quarter million members four years later.

In 1891, after a series of poor growing seasons, with farm prices the lowest ever recorded in the United States, so many farmers were forced from their land by overwhelming debts, by high prices charged by the railroads, and high interest rates for bank credit that the Populist political party, known as the "People's Party," was launched. Calling for easy credit, equitable railroads rates, and other government-subsidized policies that would aid the ailing farm population, Populist candidates were elected to Congress in scores. The defeat of the Populist presidential candidate, William Jennings Bryan, in 1896 spelled the end of the Populist ascent, and as harvests improved in the latter years of the decade, farmer discontent began to subside. The party's dissolution came about after farm prices rose.

The late nineteenth century saw the beginning of formal agricultural education with the establishment of the first agricultural college in Michigan in 1857, quickly followed by similar institutions in Maryland and Pennsylvania. The 1862 Morrill Land Grant Act gave to each state 30,000 acres of land for each senator and representative, with the purpose of endowing agricultural ("land grant") colleges. In 1892, a second Morrill Act established "separate but equal" agricultural colleges for black students, and seventeen land grant colleges for blacks opened in southern and border states.

In 1840 an Agricultural Office had been established in the U.S. Patent Office, which distributed packages of free seed to farmers. By 1854 the new office, which would become the United States Department of Agriculture, was employing a full staff— one chemist, one botanist and one entomologist—and running a five-acre experimental garden. In May 1862, Abraham Lincoln signed the bill that created an independent Department of Agriculture, dedicated to the tasks of testing and distributing plants and seeds, conducting experiments, disseminating the latest information to farmers, and collecting statistics. An early project was the study of nutritional value of foods and the ways in which nutrients were utilized by the body. Until that time it was assumed, despite the prevalence of nutritional disorders, that all food was of pretty much the same benefit, that a substantial meal of any sort satisfied the body's needs. In 1887, the Hatch Act authorized a national network of agricultural experimental stations. In 1889 the Department of Agriculture was elevated to cabinet status and the Commissioner of Agriculture became a Secretary. The county extension agent system would be established by the Smith Lever Act of 1914 to "extend" research findings to local farmers. When the boll weevil, which had crossed the Rio Grande from Mexico, threatened to destroy the booming cotton industry, agents traveled their circuits to work with farmers in combating pests and plant diseases.

The successful American farmer faced the turn of the century with confidence. He had achieved a sophisticated understanding of mortgages and credit. He was accustomed to dealing with middlemen through whom he bought and sold, with processors, bankers, transporters, and he was optimistic about his ability to supply what the market demanded, to realize a profit in the differential between his costs of production and the price he could get for his product. Between 1860 and 1900 over four hundred million acres had been added to cultivation due to the revolution in the use of farm equipment, improved transportation facilities, new scientific information, and a growing labor force of new immigrants. Domestic and foreign markets, particularly in grain and meat products, were enormously expanded. Although the largest fiber crop, cotton, had been grown in ever-increasing quantities all through the nineteenth century due to demand from England, by 1899 over a third of the crop was going to domestic mills. The booming growth in the non-agricultural population both here and abroad led to a demand for food and fibers that made the farmer of 1900 a very different man from the farmer of 1800, who grew little more than his family could consume because there was no possibility that he could dispose of his surplus at a profit.

In 1893, Jeremiah Rusk, Secretary of Agriculture under Benjamin Harrison, was concluding his four years in office. In the March issue of the *North American Review* he set forth his predictions for the next century. He felt confident that one hundred years hence we would be eating, of all things, lettuce in midwinter! He was dubious about the then fashionable notion that in the future rainfall would be controlled by explosives. He thought the idea would be abandoned along with "its twin absurdity," that other "curiosity of so-called scientific investigation . . . the flying machine." He predicted that the twentieth century would bring telephones in farmhouses, all-season roads, rural mail delivery—and that the rise in our population would call a halt to the export of food products to foreign countries. He felt that farm implements had reached their height of development although he did not discount the possibility that new inventions might be run electrically.

He concluded with a comforting message for a nation still predominantly rural. "We can all rest assured," he wrote, "that the richest inheritance a man can leave to his grandchildren and their immediate descendents will be a farm of many broad fertile acres in the United States of America."

CHAPTER VI

Boom and Bust

THE PERIOD DATING FROM THE LATE 1800s until World War I is viewed as one of the most secure in our history for the hard-working American farmer. In later years it came to be viewed as the Golden Age of agriculture. During this time farm prices rose faster than industrial prices and farm income increased proportionally. The traditionally independent farmer was learning to appreciate the value of mutual endeavor and collective action. The Federal Government had officially encouraged the farmers' cooperatives by specifying in anti-trust acts of 1914 and 1922 that they were not judged monopolies in restraint of trade. The natural hazards of farming were becoming less threatening as improved plant varieties were introduced and many plant and animal diseases were brought under control through biochemical research.

The commercial farmer of the early twentieth century had successfully adapted to an altered export market. Beginning in the 1890s overseas exports of grain and meat products had decreased due to competition for European markets from new farming regions in Russia, Argentina, Australia, and Canada. But as these exports declined domestic markets continued to expand, and supply and demand, prices and costs, remained in equilibrium. The overseas market for leaf tobacco grew as the food market declined, and cotton again became our chief export as it had been before the Civil War, despite competition from India and Egypt. An exchange of cotton for silk was developed with Japan.

Although the percentage of farmers in the labor force had decreased to approximately one third of the population, the man who worked the soil was still viewed, as he had been in Jefferson's day, as the bulwark of the state. Despite general prosperity, however, many farmers were finding the rise in land and equipment costs difficult to meet. Mortgage indebtedness had increased and so had land tenancy. Farmers who cultivated a single cash crop were particularly vulnerable financially. Fluctuating international market prices could spell disaster for a family deeply in debt for their land and equipment. Many of those who had to sell out remained as tenants on the land they once owned. Others who had started as sharecroppers and had aspired to land ownership found that rising costs doomed them and their descendants to a lifetime of land tenancy. By 1930 less than half of all farmers in the South would own the land on which they labored.

When World War I began in 1914, the aim of the American farmer was, as it had been since the mid-nineteenth century, to produce as much as he possibly could. There was no question in the minds of the farm family that a larger crop meant larger income. The farm problem was still viewed solely as a production problem. It was agreed that the government role in agriculture was to foster research and to bring the results of this research to local farmers through agricultural extension agents, who offered scientific information and practical guidance in all types of farming and livestock raising enterprises. Farmers also had come to accept another Department of Agriculture role though it was viewed more as an intrusion—the right of government to exert control over the farmer through pure food laws, grain grading, and regulations on slaughtering.

During the war there was a tremendous push for expansion of agricultural output. Food would win the war, the American farmer was told. Food was needed for our men in service and for the military and civilian populations of the allied nations, whose supplies from other allied or neutral countries were cut off by blockades, mines, and submarines. The year 1915 was notable agriculturally for the first billion-bushel wheat crop.

With increased production meeting an urgent demand, farm income rose, and so did the farmer's costs. As his sons went to war more hired help was required. The cost of freight, of fertilizer, and farm machinery went up as did the taxes on his

Cotton pickers in Georgia, 1908. LIBRARY OF CONGRESS *(following page)*

Georgia Cotton Field

land and the interest on his mortgage. Although the market was still strong, farm population began a rapid and continuing decline after 1916 as high wages in urban areas drew young men and women and marginal farmers of all ages to new forms of employment. A mass movement of southern blacks began as impoverished sharecroppers abandoned the rural South for jobs in northern cities.

When the war ended a generation of young farmers who had been released from military service returned, and many used their savings and borrowed heavily to buy farms at what proved to be peak prices. The sudden drop in export demand brought about a collapse in farm prices, and farmers were caught in a spiral of financial disaster. As they continued to produce the largest harvests possible, prices continued to fall. Those who had borrowed money to expand their land holdings saw no way to cut their production while trying to pay off their debts.

In the 1920s American farmers, alarmed by the widening gap between farm income and costs, organized to protest, and the pressure they brought to bear on legislators and administrators brought about new farm legislation in the 1930s that could scarcely have been imagined in the first two decades of the century or at any time previously.

The farm crisis had begun immediately after the World War I Armistice, due to decreased buying power in Europe. In the year 1920–21 prices received by farmers for their products fell 53 percent. All through the twenties, as other areas of the economy enjoyed prosperity, farmers, who were increasing their yield per acre annually due to efficient use of improved seed and equipment and new scientific farming methods, found that prices for their crops continued to drop.

Although several years of agricultural depression had followed all major wars in our history, the unrelieved decline in farm prices and farm income in the twenties led to a number of inconclusive Federal Government investigations and to proposals that became the basis of legislation in the thirties. The three leading farm associations, the Grange, the American Farm Bureau, and the Farmer's Union, all called for positive government action. With the advent of the Great Depression, which began with the collapse of the stock market in October 1929, farm prices dropped even more precipitously, 56 percent between 1929 and 1932. Prices of wheat were lower than they had been at any time in three hundred years. A Department of Agriculture study found average net farm income in 1932 to be $230. Many of those who were forced to abandon their farms were the "good farmers"—the modern, progressive landowners who had invested heavily in superior equipment and supplies.

In the 1932 presidential campaign, a poster urging farmers to vote for Franklin Delano Roosevelt cited his effectiveness in helping farmers while he was Governor of New York State and condemned Hoover's "record of failure." "Is the Farmer only a Third of a Man?" the poster asked over a drawing of a man in overalls being threatened by dismemberment with a huge scissors. "Six and a half million farm families—22 percent of the population—gets only 7 percent of the national income. In pay the farmer is rated a third of a man . . . The farmer's crops buy only half as much as they did before the war."

The farmers voted for Roosevelt and under his administration, known as the New Deal, a new era of government intervention in the fate of the American farmer began. The Agricultural Adjustment Act of 1933 was the first piece of New Deal legislation aimed at saving the American farm. It brought millions of farmers under voluntary contract with the Department of Agriculture and Secretary of Agriculture, Henry A. Wallace, in an agreement to reduce acreage in specific surplus crops including wheat, cotton, corn, rice, and tobacco, in return for benefit payments. That year one-quarter of the cotton crop—ten million acres—was plowed under for payments of seven to twenty dollars per acre. In essence, the government was renting the land from the farmer and letting it lie fallow, although the farmer was encouraged to plant cover crops to prevent erosion. In 1934 the Act was expanded to include such other crops considered surplus as rye, flax, barley, peanuts, sugarcane, and tobacco. The once unquestioned glorification of production gave way to the conviction that farm distress was directly related to overproduction, and farmers—many of them in a state of shocked amazement—plowed under their abundant cotton fields, their carefully nurtured corn, their golden wheat. However, the Act was not easy to police and there is no question that many farmers violated their contracts by planting on acreage theoretically retired.

The Agricultural Adjustment Act was a plan to bring production and demand into balance so that, though production *de*creased, farm prices would rise to "parity." The concept of parity—a word suggesting equality and justice—referred to prices brought by farm products during a happier, healthier agricultural era. Parity prices were established by complicated formulas based on the buying power of farm products during a time when prices received and prices paid by farmers were considered to be in balance: 1910 to 1914, the Golden Age. By enacting price support legislation, the government determined that crops grown in 1933 should bring the farmer an income with approximately the same purchasing power as it had in that earlier period. The Department of Agriculture did not offer full parity, but a percentage of parity determined by Congressional appropriations for agriculture. New developments in storage methods and facilities permitted stocking of surplus commodities until prices reached a level where the commodities could be sold at prices approaching parity.

So-called "non-recourse" loans were made to farmers in 1933 for their corn and cotton crops at 50 percent of parity for corn and 69 percent of parity for cotton. The farmer received the money and when the corn was ready for harvest he was entitled to sell it on the open market at a higher price if prices had risen and repay the government for the loan. If the commodity did not reach the price of the loan he could simply turn over his crop in payment to the newly formed Commodity Credit Corporation and the government would consider the loan repaid. In 1938 payments were offered to producers of corn, cotton, rice, tobacco, and wheat that were as close to parity as funding permitted. Surplus commodities were distributed to the needy through food stamp and school lunch programs.

The Agricultural Adjustment Act was declared unconstitutional in 1936 because it infringed on states' rights but its basic functions were carried forth under other legislation such as the Soil Conservation and Domestic Allotment Acts. A second Agricultural Adjustment Act was passed in 1938 allotting a certain amount of acreage for a given commodity to each state. The states and counties then assigned it to individual farmers. Under the act farmers received parity payments, acreage allotment payments, and payments for carrying on specified conservation practices. Other New Deal legislation attacked problems of soil and water conservation, expanded farm credit, offered aid to marginal farmers and to tenant farmers seeking to acquire land, and brought electricity to rural areas.

Today, when most farm families expect and enjoy virtually the same comforts and conveniences available to the urban population, it is difficult to realize that, although the gaslight era ended in the cities in 1882, only 9.5 percent of farms had electricity by 1929. The Rural Electrification Act of 1935 made low interest loans to local electric cooperatives and private utilities so that they could extend electric power lines to rural areas. By 1947 half of all farm families had electricity, although only one third had inside toilets and central heating. It was not until 1965 that 98 percent of farm homes were equipped with electricity and could enjoy such basic and commonplace benefits as electric lights, washing machines, refrigerators, cooking stoves, as well as efficient farm equipment like the milking machine.

Other acts, including the Resettlement Administration and the Farm Security Administration, offered rehabilitation aid and funding for farm families and were successful in helping many of the poor to stay on the land, in helping new farmers get a start, and in encouraging cooperatives. The entire complex of New Deal programs succeeded in raising net farm income 50 percent between 1932 and 1935, but although many farmers were enabled to hold onto their land, 750,000 landowners lost their farms, their homes, and a lifetime of savings and investment through foreclosures and bankruptcy between 1930 and 1935. It was not until 1941, when the country was again plunged into a wartime economy favorable to agriculture, that farm income rose as high as it had been during 1929.

The innovative legislation of the 1930s, which offered relief to so many desperate American farmers, failed to help most of the very neediest, the marginal small farmer, who did not grow a crop considered surplus, and the tenant farmer or sharecropper. As farmers with large landholdings received direct payments from government under acreage retirement (or plowing-under) programs, many were also able to gain a double return from their land by devoting former cotton or wheat acreage to soybeans or other nonrestricted crops. The small diversified farmer or the farmer who was already devoting his land to non-restricted crops was not entitled to such benefits. For the tenant farmer, particularly those growing cotton, which was always highly subject to fluctuations in the world market, government subsidies led to evictions. Landowners, who were restricted to smaller acreage or whose land had been eroded by dust storms, replaced the men, women, and children, who provided their labor, and their horses and mules, with efficient new tractors. Between 1930 and 1937 the sale of farm tractors in ten cotton-growing states increased 90 percent.

John Steinbeck's powerful novel, *The Grapes of Wrath,* which dramatized for readers all over the country the tragic plight of the southern sharecropper and which later became an equally popular film, begins as Tom Joad, released from three years in prison, hitches a ride to his family's home, a farm they once owned but now sharecrop. He tells the driver, " '. . . my old man got a place, forty acres. He's a cropper but we been there a long time.'

"The driver looked significantly at the fields along the road where the corn was fallen sideways and the dust was piled on it. Little flints showed through the dusty soil. The driver said, as though to himself, 'A forty-acre cropper and he ain't been dusted out and ain't been tractored out?' "

Tom learns that the man's uneasiness is well-founded. He arrives as the family is preparing to leave, with all their possessions loaded in a decrepit truck. They are heading for California, where they expect to find work picking fruit. " 'It's dirt hard for folks to tear up an' go,' " Tom's father says later to other migrants. " 'Folks like us that had our place. We ain't shif'less. Till we got tractored off, we was people with a farm.' "

In 1935 tenancy rates, particularly in the South, had reached new highs. Although only 6 percent of the farmers in Massachusetts were listed as tenants, in Mississippi the figure was 70 percent. Nationwide white tenants outnumbered blacks, but in the South the numbers were about equal. The American dream of independence through land ownership was pure fan-

Loading hay in Door County, Wisconsin, 1940. LIBRARY OF CONGRESS

tasy to these black and white families who lived in similar conditions of impoverishment.

The Farm Security Administration, which launched a comprehensive attack on rural poverty, found that in Mississippi, Alabama, and Arkansas, in 1934, tenant income averaged $132 for a family per year. The roads in the cotton belt were clogged with croppers on the move carrying their few possessions, searching for a more promising situation. Most continued to descend the economic scale with each uprooting. In 1935 it was found that two-thirds of southern tenant farmers had been on their present land less than a year.

Northern observers wrote shocking descriptions of southern tenant farm families who lived in rickety leaky shacks with no plumbing and often no outhouse. They described homes in which there was virtually nothing to eat, where everyone worked all day in the fields including children as young as six, and where such diseases as pellagra, malaria, and hookworm resulted from inadequate diet, lack of sanitation, and being barefoot.

Erskine Caldwell, who visited Georgia, gave this description in a series of articles he wrote in *The New York Post.*

> In one room a six-year-old boy licked the paper bag the meat had been brought in. His legs were scarcely any larger than a medium sized dog's legs . . . suffering from rickets and anemia his legs were unable to carry him more than a dozen steps at a time; suffering from malnutrition his belly was swollen several times its normal size. His face was bony and white. He was starving to death.

Writer James Agee and photographer Walker Evans stayed at the homes of three sharecropper families in Alabama. In their book, *Let Us Now Praise Famous Men,* Agee describes the barefoot women and their garments, which were most often dresses made from fertilizer sacks.

> Wide hemmed holes cut for the arms, no collar; a wide triangle cut for nursing and hemmed in coarse stitching like the armholes; a broad skirt reaching about two inches below the knee, and falling in thick folds; the

Sharecropper's daughter near Whitestone, South Carolina, 1941.
LIBRARY OF CONGRESS

grain of the cloth defined here and there in dark grease; the whole garment clayed and sweated; the faded yet bold trademarks showing through in unexpected parts of the material.

Recollections of these terrible times continue to appear. In a recently published book, *A Childhood,* writer Harry Crewes recalls his early years in southern Georgia in the 1930s. His father, whose grandfather had owned a large plantation run by slaves, worked as a sharecropper. "The farm had sixty acres in cultivation, and so Luther Carter furnished Uncle John and daddy each a mule. Thirty acres was as much as one man and one mule could tend, and even then they had to step smart from first sun to last to do it. They had no cows or hogs and no smokehouse, and that first year they lived—as we did for much of my childhood—on fatback, grits, tea without ice, and biscuits made from flour and water and lard." The first year the tobacco crop failed: "What this meant was that in August at the end of the crop year he got half of nothing. They stayed alive on what they could borrow against the coming crop and what little help they could find from their people, who had not done well that year either."

In Arkansas, where cotton plantations were relatively recently established on former swampland, a group of sharecroppers formed the Southern Tenant Farmers Union and protested the Agricultural Adjustment Administration's lack of concern with the plight of tenant farmers. The group, originally made up of eleven white and seven black sharecroppers in an area of the country where blacks and whites customarily did not mingle, brought suit against their landowners for refusing to share the payments for crop reduction by the federal government. Although the law provided for such sharing there was little enforcement and landlords were permitted to deduct old debts before making disbursement. In many cases they both withheld payment and ousted tenants.

The suit was lost but new locals were formed, and for the first time in anyone's experience, black and white farmers, equally vulnerable to exploitation, joined to fight for their rights, paying ten cents a month in dues or nothing, if they had

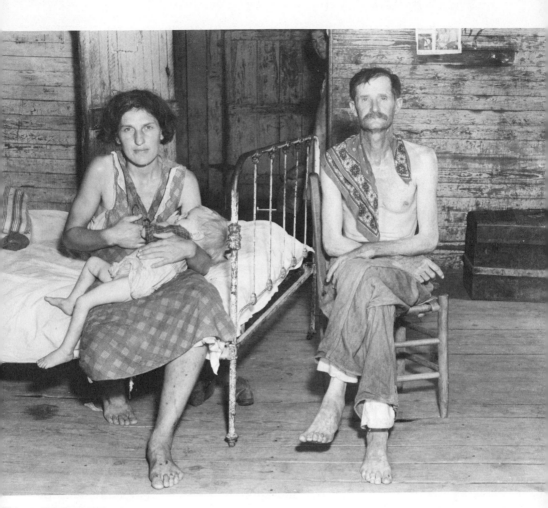

Sharecropper family in Hale County, Alabama, 1936. LIBRARY OF
CONGRESS

nothing. The Union grew to include five thousand members who called for a halt to evictions, of forced buying and selling through plantation commissaries, of direct payment of crop-reduction benefits by the Federal government. They asked for representation on local control boards and called for cooperation between black and white farmers.

The agitations in Arkansas made national news when farmers picketed in front of the Department of Agriculture in Washington. Norman Thomas, six times the Socialist Party candidate for president, visited Arkansas and in radio broadcasts described the tenants as "The forgotten men of the New Deal," saying, "the AAA has done nothing for the sharecropper . . . the landlord gets the money and the sharecropper gets the air." Later legislation attempted to assist tenant farmers in their struggle for fair treatment, and today's National Sharecropper's Fund, which is an outgrowth of the Southern Tenant Farmer's Union and which developed in conjunction with anti-poverty and civil rights efforts in 1962, has continued the struggle to help poor farmers who want to stay on the land.

The dust storms of the 1930s, which devastated fifty million acres of land in Oklahoma, Texas, Kansas, and the Dakotas, sent an endless stream of refugees, like the fictional Joad family, off to California to seek work. In the Plains States of the West, where homesteaders had settled early in the twentieth century after the closing of the frontier, much of the land was unsuitable for anything but grazing. Rainfall was light and strong winds stirred the long grass where herds grazed, "the buffalo roamed, and the deer and antelope played." The homesteaders plowed up the strong grasses, which had saved the land from erosion, and planted wheat and cotton. For many favorable years the crops grew, and then, in the middle thirties, the land, which in good years enjoyed ten to twenty inches of rainfall compared with seventy-five in the Pacific Northwest and forty to fifty in the northern Atlantic region, became parched through prolonged droughts. The topsoil began to blow and a series of dust storms carried off soil, seed, and plants from the dry land with no protective cover.

In the *Saturday Evening Post* a South Dakota observer wrote: "By midmorning a gale was blowing, cold and black. By noon

96

it was blacker than night because one can see through night and this was opaque black. It was a wall of dirt one's eyes could not penetrate, but it could penetrate the eyes and ears and nose . . . If a person was outside, he tied his handkerchief around his face, but he still coughed up black . . . When the wind died and the sun shown forth again, it was on a different world. There were no fields, only sand drifting into mounds and eddies . . . In the farmyard, fences, machinery and trees were gone, buried. The roofs of sheds stuck out through drifts deeper than a man is tall."

The storms continued as farmland took on the appearance of sand dunes. Frederick Lewis Allen, in his book *Since Yesterday,* noted that dust storms were attributed to the Lord, who was playing a joke on the AAA, as the Agricultural Adjustment Act was called. "So it's crop reduction you want, is it? I'll show you."

The dust storm emigrés, derisively known as "Okies," found scant work in California, where, since 1870, vast growing areas of a thousand acres or more had been worked by tenants and hired labor from China, Japan, the Philippines, Mexico, and other foreign countries. Three hundred thousand of these white Protestant indigents huddled together in shantytowns referred to as "Little Oklahomas." By 1938, 221,000 dust bowl migrants were counted in California. Steinbeck described the emigrés as they arrived: ". . . their hunger was in their eyes, and their need was in their eyes. They had no argument, no system, nothing but their numbers and their needs. When there was work for a man ten men fought for it—fought with a low wage. If that fella'll work for thirty cents, I'll work for twenty-five. If he'll take twenty five, I'll do it for twenty. No, me, I'm hungry. I'll work for fifteen. I'll work for food. The kids. You ought to see them. Little boils, like, comin' out, an' they can't run aroun'. Give 'em some windfall fruit an' they bloated up. Me. I'll work for a little piece of meat."

When World War II began, the majority of these displaced farmers went to the cities and found work in defense plants. Few returned home to the dust bowl, where, according to a bitter contemporary joke, the land was "so barren that when a jackrabbit goes out for a run he carries lunch."

An abandoned farmstead shows the disastrous effects of wind erosion.
UNITED STATES DEPARTMENT OF AGRICULTURE *(following page)*

The dust storms were not the only highly damaging natural disasters of the 1930s. In 1936 there were floods along the Merrimack, Connecticut, Hudson, Delaware, Susquehanna, Potomac, Allegheny, and Ohio rivers, which resulted in numerous flood control, anti-erosion and other conservation projects. The Soil Conservation Service set up demonstration projects in farming communities. Unemployed men aged eighteen to twenty-five were recruited for CCC (Civilian Conservation Corps) camps to fight erosion and fertility depletion. The Tennessee Valley Authority began earlier, in 1933, to salvage 8.5 million acres of land in Tennessee and six other states through which the Tennessee River ran. Seven million acres had been severely damaged by erosion, and 4.5 million people, most of them farm families, lived in poverty. The TVA built dams, generated electricity for these dams, stopped the silting and flooding of the area.

World War II ended the Great Depression. As a wartime economy again raised prices and the unemployed went back to work, farm prices, which stood at 77 percent of parity in 1939, rose to full parity and above. The labor shortage on farms during the war brought about the final transition from animal power to tractor power. By 1940 hybrid corn, developed in 1925 by Donald Jones at the Connecticut State Experimental Station, had been planted throughout the corn belt, radically increasing yields. Fewer and fewer farms and farmers have been involved in the decades since in our massive production of food and fiber. In the late 1930s the number of farms in this country peaked at 6.8 million. Since then we have lost 4 million farms and doubled our agricultural production. As tax-funded research has continued to concentrate on increasing crop yields, agricultural surpluses have been a major problem. Each succeeding administration has attempted to cope with surplus disposal, with bolstering farm income, with new issues brought about by an evolving modern technology. The multi-faceted "farm problem" has been a persistent source of distress to the President, the Secretary of Agriculture, to congressmen, to hard-pressed farmers, and to the scowling little figure in the political cartoons who is intended to represent us all and is labeled TAXPAYER.

CHAPTER VII
Where We Stand

Since the 1940s farming in this country has changed so radically and rapidly that we refer to the period as one of revolution. Forty years ago one in four Americans lived on a farm. Today fewer than 5 percent of us are members of farm families. Forty years ago, when production was half what it is today, there were as many horses as tractors providing "horsepower" on the farm. Today agriculture is totally mechanized and, in certain specialities such as sugarcane and chicken broiler production, so highly industrialized that an agricultural operation may resemble a factory assembly line more than it does most people's image of farming.

Farms have become fewer and larger as successful farmers seek more land to fully utilize their expensive equipment—often buying out their less successful neighbors. Farms have also become less diversified because it is more profitable to grow a large acreage of one or two crops using specialized machinery to plant, cultivate, and harvest than it is to care for a variety of crops and livestock. As the number of small farms steadily plummeted between surveys made in 1960 and 1974, the number of farms earning over $100,000 annually in gross receipts increased five times. It is generally acknowledged today that an essential factor in profitable farming is the substitution of capital for labor, and the farmer who does not have the financial resources to acquire the necessary equipment and the land required to make the equipment pay is unable to compete and often unable to survive. It is estimated that, if current trends encouraging bigness persist, 40 percent or approximately another 1 million of our 2.7 million farms will be lost by the year 2000.

How did these changes come about? If the family farm seems

101

to be going the way of the family-owned corner grocery store perhaps, as some people believe, this is an economic inevitability, regrettable only on sentimental grounds. And yet, a growing number of critics point to the fact that the rapid expansion of industrialized farming has led to an insupportable consumption of energy, has accelerated soil degradation, polluted the air and the water, and tainted the food we eat. The loss of millions of family farmers has undermined rural and small town economies, which depend for their vitality and survival on local farmers who buy locally, spend locally, and have a compelling interest in local social and political life. When their land is taken over by large corporate farming ventures with absentee owners who acquire their supplies elsewhere, local merchants cannot survive. For every six family farms that sell out one small-town business folds.

The definition of a family farm has nothing to do with chickens scratching outside the back door, with apple pies baking in the oven, with the sound of the scythe cutting through the hayfield. The accepted definition for census purposes also does not relate to farm size or farm income. What it means is an owner-operated enterprise for which the family makes the decisions, provides the labor, and does not employ a manager or use more than 1.5 man years of hired labor. Land ownership is not required by the definition, and many family farmers own part of their land and lease additional acreage. Some find that due to the high cost of land today it is more profitable for them to lease *all* of their acreage and some farmers lease equipment as well.

A family farm may be a small truck farm or, since mechanization has made this possible, a vast spread of grain. It may be a ten-acre tobacco allotment, a twelve-hundred acre corn and soybean operation, a small diversified crop and livestock holding, a fifty-acre apple orchard or citrus grove. Newspaper and magazine articles seeking for the "typical" farm family of today may feature a happy, vigorous, and prosperous middle-aged man shown considering the purchase of a $100,000 center pivot irrigation machine that moves automatically across the field, or driving his air conditioned 150-horsepower tractor with CB and AM-FM radios, or reading computer printouts analyzing

Louise Swanson, a senior at the University of Minnesota, handles a 4-bottom plow with ease. UNITED STATES DEPARTMENT OF AGRICULTURE

his production results. He sends all his children to college and takes his wife on European vacations. Other articles show a young couple struggling to grow, by organic methods, a wide variety of vegetables or an old man tending hogs on the land his great grandfather farmed.

What we *can* say about the typical American farmer, if we look at the surveys, is that he is not the young pioneer of Jefferson's day but a man of fifty to fifty-five, whose children are unlikely to follow in his footsteps. He is less dependent than his father was on family labor and much more dependent on suppliers, on financiers, on petroleum resources. Whereas his father kept workhorses and fueled them with grain raised in his fields, today's farmer knows that his productivity and ability to compete are directly related to his level of technological knowledge, his skill in financial management, and the efficient use of his equipment. The average farmer is still a self-employed entrepreneur, but, since the cost of production necessities such as machinery, feed, and fertilizer have skyrocketed along with the price of agricultural land, expenses now take as much as 75 cents of every dollar he earns.

Farming has changed and farmers have changed. The old jokes about the "country bumpkin" and the "city slicker" have lost their meaning as farmers have become more like urban people in their tastes and manners. New highways have given rural people easy access to urban areas; television keeps farm families abreast of happenings at home and abroad and provides an entertainment and education medium shared with city people. More and more farmers have attended college and bring to their work the latest technological and managerial expertise. Even in the remote hollows of the southern Appalachians, where poor hill farmers commonly lived out their lives without even having visited the county seat, advances in transportation and education have transformed the experiences and expectations of the young.

The contemporary farmer, who can rarely set the price on what he buys or on what he sells, who has usually lost direct contact with the consumer, often describes himself as a man who "buys retail and sells wholesale" and as a man who "lives poor and dies rich." The National Farmer's Union has esti-

Farmer seeding winter wheat, 1957. UNITED STATES DEPARTMENT OF AGRICULTURE

mated that a man earning only $10,000 a year from his farm is likely to leave an estate valued at over $300,000. His land is his primary asset, but unless he is to quit farming and sell out he himself cannot realize the wealth this real estate represents. And although his land may be a fine legacy for his children, they will find if they continue to farm that as the cost of farm production keeps climbing the income potential of the land will diminish further.

The family farmer views as his competitor both his more prosperous neighbor and an impersonal giant referred to as "the corporate farm." Although the term "corporate farm" is generally used to mean a large-scale operation run by hired managers and controlled by stockholders of considerable wealth who may live in other states or even in other countries, most corporate farms are actually held by family corporations. Incorporation eases taxes in the transfer of land through inheritance, offers income tax reductions, and improved opportunities for financing. Some family corporations own extensive operations, but even small farms may be incorporated with shares held by family members.

The large corporate farms, which are commonly seen as the enemies of the family farm, are also often described as "factory farms" or "industrial farms" because, as in manufacturing, they are run by managers or foremen who supervise large crews of laborers using the latest equipment. They may also employ assembly-line techniques by which produce is picked, packaged, boxed, and sent off by truck to distribution centers. These vast farms, without farmhouses, are particularly prominent in the production of sugarcane, broiler chickens and citrus fruits. Industrialized farms have a virtual monopoly in certain vegetable crops, such as tomatoes grown to be canned, where production is often tied in with processing. They are also the rule on feed lots, where thousands of heads of cattle are fattened and sometimes also slaughtered. California, Texas, and Florida are the states where these industrialized farms are most heavily concentrated.

The term "agribusiness" refers to the complex of industries that produces farm inputs such as fertilizer, seed, and machinery and that may also be involved in food processing, distribution, and transport. Today the industries involved in the supply of agricultural products and the many industries that bring the food to the consumer employ three times the number of people as work on farms. A conglomerate involved in these enterprises may become directly involved in growing by purchasing and managing farmland. It may also contract with local growers or livestock raisers to buy their produce at a negotiated price at a time and price related to their handling, processing, and storage schedules and capacities. Such contract farming can be beneficial to the farmer. Since a buyer for his produce is guaranteed his risk is lessened. But contract farming also separates ownership, operation, and management and reduces the actual farm owner to an often underpaid employee of the processor. As the Family Farm Commission of the North Dakota Farmer's Union expressed it in a recent report: "The farmer's once independent role is progressively that of a piece-worker in an assembly line."

Although many people fear a complete takeover of the nation's agriculture by the conglomerates, it is not correct to suggest that this is happening now, and, in fact, a number of conglomerates have sold off their farming interests in recent years because they proved unprofitable. Still, there is no question about the fact that the large corporate farm offers unfair competition to local farmers. Their farming endeavors may actually be run at a loss with losses written off against gains in other areas of their business. Large operations also receive cheaper inputs because of advantages in purchasing machinery and supplies in large quantities, and in easier credit terms. They are also the farms that employ crews of migratory workers, who receive lower wages than does a local hired hand employed by a family farm. Currently the largest 6 percent of our farms, those with an annual income of over $100,000, account for 52 percent of all farm sales, according to recent USDA figures.

It is not easy, when so much that is written on the subject presents conflicting evidence, to perceive whether the institution of the family farm is still thriving or is rapidly dying out. The most recent census counts 90 percent of our farms as family farms, although they account for less than half of the total farm output. Most diversified farming takes place on family farms, and they are also prominent in grain production, tobacco raising, and dairying. Despite the fact that the average farmer earns a lower income than his friends in non-farm occupations, many farm families enjoy a high standard of living.

Pessimism about the future of the family farm is, however, well-founded. It is based on the constantly decreasing share of farm profits small and medium-sized farms receive and on the fact that so few young men and women are able to become farmers unless they inherit a substantial farm and have the technical and financial skills required by modern agriculture. Farms that have an annual gross sale of under $20,000 still account for 72 percent of all farms, although they receive only 11 percent of the cash receipts from farming. Over half of all farm families live on farms that earn less than $10,000 in gross receipts, and most minority farmers fit into this category. In 1930 fewer than one in six farms were worked part time, but today most small farmers and their families take outside jobs to supplement their income, and the major part of their income is most often derived from these off-farm jobs.

Although the incidence of poverty among farm families is considerably lower than it was a decade ago, due primarily to the movement of poor farmers to the cities, an estimated 12 to 20 percent of the small farm population has total income below the poverty line. Farm poverty shows regional distribution, with over half of those in this category living in the southeastern part of the country. President Lyndon Johnson's 1967 commission on rural poverty found in its report, titled "The People Left Behind," that a high percentage of the men and women in urban slums came from rural slums, having left the farm ill-equipped for other types of employment.

It is difficult to imagine that aspiring farmers would take heart from such figures, particularly those who do not have a farm in the family where they can work with parents or siblings or which they might some day inherit. According to recent Government Accounting Office figures, starting a moderate-sized family farm now requires $250,000 to $575,000 for land and equipment. In 1940, when one in four Americans lived on a farm, the average real estate value of a farm was $5,000. Today prime farmland often sells for from $1200 to as much as $3000 an acre, with an average cost of $1500 in 1978. The study also found, to nobody's surprise, that financial institutions are more likely to loan to investors and to well-established farmers than to new farmers who might be attempting to purchase the same piece of land.

Once a young farmer has attained credit to start a farm he and his wife are likely to have to work it part time while holding down city jobs as factory workers, bus drivers, office workers. The stress of trying to make a farm produce efficiently while attempting to earn enough to keep up farm expenses and payments by working at another full-time job has defeated courageous and able farmers in all parts of the country.

In addition to luck, access to credit, and a willingness to work eighteen hours a day if necessary, today's young farmer must become a marketing specialist if he is to get the best prices for his crops so that he will be able to keep up payments on his farm and equipment. Because of changes in the Federal farm laws in 1973 most crops are now sold on the private market. The government no longer buys and stores crops, with the exception of food destined for foreign aid and school lunch programs or for surplus commodity distributions to the poor. Although the government will make cash payments to farmers if the prices on the market fall below "target prices" set by the government, farmers are expected to do their own storing until crops reach desired prices. They are offered low-interest loans for erecting storage facilities and in the Midwest in particular the new galvanized metal storage bins are a conspicuous feature of the landscape. The novice farmer, who is invariably in debt for his land and machinery, must decide whether to sell his entire crop at harvest time or whether to store his crop and wait for a rise in prices. He may decide to sell most of his crop in the fall, but for income tax purposes take payment in January. He may also, of course, guess wrong and miss the peak, having to pay for storage while selling at low prices later in the year.

We read of high farm prices in the newspapers and fear that higher prices will mean much higher food costs to the consumer. What we are not told often is that only 39 percent of the price of food sold in our supermarkets goes to the farmer. The many ways in which a farmer can go bankrupt are even less often explored, but these simple and distressing calculations appeared in a recent article on the subject. A capable young farmer was able to purchase top quality farmland in the Midwest at $1800 an acre with a 9 percent loan. He found that, although he was growing 110 bushels of corn per acre and receiving $2 a bushel, his cost to grow an acre of corn was $100. His profit, therefore, was only $120 an acre and the annual interest on his loan came to $160 per acre. He was also expected to pay off part of the principal of his loan each year.

Those concerned about the future of the family farm point with blame at the Federal Government. Although the family farm has always officially been the prime objective of public policy, the large farmer receives the major share of government benefits because subsidies are geared to the volume of production, and he often uses these funds to acquire additional land and equipment. Between 1964 and 1974 the 20 percent of farmers in the highest income group received half of all government payments. Some regions of the country, such as the corn, cotton, and wheat belts, have benefited considerably more than other sections, and farms in these areas have become increasingly large and specialized.

This has not gone without notice—or implied regret. In 1950 President Dwight D. Eisenhower said in a speech to Congress:

> The chief beneficiaries of our price support programs have been the two million larger, highly mechanized farming units which produce about 85 percent of our agricultural output. The individual production of the remaining farms, numbering about 3.5 million, is so small that the farmer derives little benefit from price supports.

But three decades later government policy remains essentially unchanged and we have lost 2.8 million small and medium-sized farms.

Eleven years after Eisenhower's address, the Agricultural Act of 1961 stated: "It is hereby declared to be the policy of Congress . . . to recognize the importance of the family farm as an efficient unit of production and as an economic base for towns and cities in rural areas, to encourage, promote, and strengthen this form of farm enterprise."

And yet government programs continued to assist large farmers grow larger, and the number of small and medium-sized farms continued to decline.

Farming, with the exception of national defense, is the only major sector of our economy that is subsidized by the government, but the long range results of programs designed in the 1930s, when most farmers were in distress and the government stepped in to rescue them from bankruptcy, has been to help the big farmer become bigger. Although it has been considered a matter of public interest that farm income should keep pace with industrial income, that society should share some of the risks of farming, that the government should help buffer the fluctuations in supply and demand that make farming such an insecure form of livelihood, government programs under succeeding administrations have given most help to those who have needed it least.

The farmer is the only member of society who is paid not to produce. Acreage retirement plans have always been unpopular in a world in which hunger is widespread, and such current plans place farmers with limited acreage on which to earn their living at a disadvantage, even if they are subsidized by the government, as compared with those who can easily afford to keep 10 to 20 percent of the farmland temporarily out of production. The 1977 Farm Act continued to emphasize crop limitations with increased price supports.

Federal tax laws, although they were designed to have the opposite effect, have also promoted the trend away from the small family-owned farm. The highest income-level farmers and investors are particularly encouraged by such tax shelters as accelerated depreciation on machinery and equipment, agricultural tax credits, and provisions for reducing taxes by converting farm income into capital gains. The smaller farmer gets much less advantage from these provisions.

The result of all this is that less than half the farmland in this country is now owned by the person who actually does the work. The rest is farmed by individual tenants, who find that renting land is more economical than owning land, and by large corporate farming enterprises.

There is another factor that has influenced the current distribution of our farmland, along with price support programs and tax laws. In recent decades the focus of tax-supported agricultural research has been technologies suitable to large-scale farming. The square, thick-walled tomato developed for mechanical harvesting is a typical example. It is the result of research aimed at engineering food products to fit the requirements of industrialized farming. Only a very small percentage of tax dollars allotted to investigations at land grant colleges and state agricultural research stations has been directed toward methods and technologies that can be used by small and medium-sized farms.

Meanwhile, the average farmer complains—and persists. It is not easy for the outsider to understand what rewards farming brings that make the risks worthwhile. Farmer Joe Johnson and his brother Bill farm 268 acres and care for a dairy herd on land the family has owned for 209 years and that is now within the city limits of Manassas, Virginia. While milking the cows one morning at 5:30 with their sons, one of the brothers answered this central question asked by a *Washington Post* reporter: "Not too many jobs I can think of where you can work close with your kids. You look at these boys working with the livestock and you realize they develop a sense of responsibility that'd be hard to teach anyplace else."

In Studs Terkel's book, *Working,* an Illinois farmer named Pierce Walker explains it this way:

> Farming, it's such a gamble. The weather and the prices and everything that goes with it . . . You have so many days to get the crop planted and the same in the fall to harvest it . . . You try to beat the weather. It tenses you up. Whether we need rain or we don't need rain, it affects you in different ways . . . When you get a good crop that's more or less your reward. If you weren't proud of your work, you wouldn't have no place on the farm. 'Cause you don't work by the hour. And you put in a lot of hours, I tell ya.

CHAPTER VIII

Can We Save the Family Farm?

Although the income on the family farm has, all through our history, been lower than non-farm income, recent public protests by farmers have thrust the urgency of the cost-price squeeze before the American public. In December of 1977 and again in February of 1979 farmer's tractorcades under the banner of the recently formed American Agricultural Movement traveled from distant states to Washington, D.C. to bring their demands for increases in price supports to the White House and Congress.

Most of the members of the A.A.M., who came to Washington to demonstrate in front of the capitol, owned medium-sized farms in the grain growing areas of the country. Many of these distressed farmers had been considerably more prosperous when unfavorable weather abroad and sharply increased export demand led to a boom in farm prices in the years 1973 to 75. Encouraged by government programs they borrowed money to increase their acreage and invested heavily in additional equipment. Wheat prices then fell from a high of $6 a bushel to $1.80 a bushel as costs of production rose 50 percent. At the time of the protests farmers were earning $2.50 a bushel on wheat that cost $3.50 a bushel to raise. Older farmers, many of whom had paid off loans on land and equipment, found themselves able to survive the crisis but the younger farmers, saddled with high bank loan payments, were severely threatened.

As government farm policies continue to excite controversy, all the major farm organizations—the Farm Bureau, the National Grange, the National Farmer's Union, and the much smaller National Farmer's Organization—agree that efforts to preserve the family farm should be a priority of the U.S. De-

113

Farmers' protest, Washington, D.C., February, 1979. JOSHUA HORWITZ

partment of Agriculture, and all agree that this is not presently the case.

Since government policies of the past four decades have led to increasing concentration of land holdings, in a country historically committed to broad distribution of small holdings, suggestions for federal and state programs that will halt the trend toward fewer and larger farms are emerging from farmer's organizations, from public interest groups, from government agencies, and from individuals. All see the "corporate invasion" of agriculture as undesirable—not only for the average farmer and his children but for the American public. Some of these suggestions for legal, political, and educational action have already been recognized in new laws and have led to the founding of new organizations specifically dedicated to the preservation of the family farm; others are opposed by powerful interest groups and are not likely to be realized.

It is generally recognized that if the family farm is to be saved, government programs and benefits must be retargeted to assist smaller and more diversified farms. One suggestion is that a limit be put on the number of bushels on which the farmer can receive direct payments or loans. Such limits would remove a major incentive for expansion. Currently sixteen states, in an attempt to protect local farmers, have enacted or are considering some type of anti-corporate farm legislation, many of them allowing corporate farms only under certain conditions related to residency, size of farm, and number of stockholders. Most permit incorporation of family farms that remain family operated.

Many people favor laws that would prevent further foreign investment in farmland, but the fact is that American farmland has become an immensely popular investment among wealthy Europeans, Middle Easterners, and Asians. The declining value of the dollar and the fact that prime farmland is twice as expensive in Western Europe as it is here led to the purchase of 80 million dollars worth of U.S. farmland by foreign nationals in 1978. Many were able to take advantage of tax benefits as well by investing through corporations with headquarters in such places as the Dutch Antilles where little or no income tax need be paid.

115

Another suggestion commonly made is that government-funded research and information programs be redirected toward the problems of smaller farmers. Research, for instance, could cease focusing on technology requiring high capitalization and high energy consumption and focus on the development of small-scale, energy-efficient machinery and on organic farming. The U.S. Department of Agriculture set aside 3 million dollars in 1979 for research related to small farms—a small but significant sum—and also offered 3 percent loans for farm purchase and improvement to qualified "limited resource" farmers through the Farmer's Home Administration. Other programs helped small farmers participate in cost-sharing conservation programs formerly only available to those with larger resources. On the state level, several states have initiated extension programs to assist low income farmers. Many are based on the pioneering Missouri Small Farm Program which employs retired and part-time farmers and sends them out into the field to offer farm management and production advice to the state's predominantly small farmers.

There are a number of ways in which tax laws could be changed to reduce the advantages now given to agribusiness, to large corporate farms, and to land speculators. Many of these proposals would, at the same time, increase the advantages to those who make a living only in farming. Most of us accept the idea of the graduated income tax, in which those who make a greater income are taxed at a higher rate than those of low income. Some states are now considering a progressive property tax on farmland which would, in a similar fashion, tax large properties at a higher rate than small ones. In some states tax credits are offered to those developing solar and other alternative energy sources. Although no one believes that the American farmer should abandon the use of machinery and fossil fuel and return to the mule-drawn plow, soaring energy costs have led to small farm projects around the country encouraging experimentation with energy saving techniques. Suggestions for raising farm income while cutting production costs through use of alternative energy sources include generating methane gas from manure, engineering wind-powered irrigation systems, and solar heated farmhouses and barns.

116

Changes are already taking place in estate tax laws to make it easier to pass on a family farm to the next generation. Valuation of farmland has been so high heirs often had to sell much of their inheritance to pay estate taxes. New laws value land at its capacity for agricultural profits rather than at its inflated market value or potential value for real estate development. Inheritance tax discrimination against farm women has been effectively opposed in recent years. Some changes have been made and others are pending in laws that left a farm widow at a severe disadvantage if her husband predeceased her. Although the family farm might have been jointly held by husband and wife, laws required that the widow prove actual contributions of money toward the purchase or development of the land without recognition of the fact that the average farm wife shares fully in the labor of the farm, makes many of the decisions, may do part or all of the record keeping and accounting.

A typical case was reported recently by Common Cause, a widely based citizen's group that seeks to bring urgent problems before the public.

> I worked along-side my husband, Floyd, for 33 years. Together we'd built up a ranch of 3,400 acres and 120 cows. I'd done everything on the ranch, feeding the pigs, milking the cows, driving the tractor. Two years before he died, Floyd was all crippled up so I had to do everything, with the two boys who were still in school . . . Then Floyd died in 1974 and I found out I had to pay $23,000 in inheritance tax for my own ranch. We were already in debt about $40,000 . . . If I had died instead of Floyd, he wouldn't have had to pay any tax . . . I didn't get any credit for my work on the ranch all those years. If I chose to work on the ranch, why should that be worth less than going to town and getting a job?"

Other cases cited in *Farm Journal* include that of a woman who ran the farm entirely on her own during an eighteen year period when her husband was disabled. The court held that the land and income produced by the farm were the property of the husband at the time of his death and therefore subject to the

117

usual inheritance tax. A bill drafted by Senator Gaylord Nelson would virtually eliminate the "widow's tax" by giving farm wives credit for their assistance in running the operation.

Champions of the family farm want inheritance taxes structured to facilitate the passage of family-held farms to other family members as well as widows. Many also propose that—to avoid the development in this country of a landed gentry class like that which typified the societies the colonists fled—taxes be written to encumber inheritance of very large concentrations of land.

Several states are now passing laws that would increase the availability of capital and credit to applicants who are proven to be capable farmers. A number of states are now discussing programs modeled on the Minnesota Family Farm Security Act of 1976 which offers state-guaranteed loans from a special fund to well-motivated farmers who have less than $50,000 in assets.

A widespread movement to encourage cooperatives is based on enabling poor farmers to lower their costs and raise their bargaining power. Although most financially sound independent farmers belong to one or more cooperatives, it has proven difficult to organize co-ops for low-income farmers. Under New Deal legislation the Banks for Cooperatives attempted to deal with the problem, but this program like so many others found success with large farmers rather than with the most needy. In 1935 the Farm Security Agency was able to establish thousands of small local marketing cooperatives for black and white southern farms. But the agency was abolished in 1945.

The current poor people's co-op movement traces its roots to the civil rights activism of the 1960s and is led by the Southern Cooperative Development Fund, which was founded by the National Sharecroppers Fund, the Office of Economic Opportunity, and the Southern Regional Council. Farmers and co-op managers are being trained near Epes, Alabama at the Rural Training, Research, and Demonstration Farming Center which opened in 1970. The National Sharecropper's Fund runs a training program, directed toward the needs of small farmers, at the Frank P. Graham Experimental Farm and Training Center near Wadesboro, North Carolina, where techniques suitable for farmers with limited capital are promoted. Emphasis is placed on the fact that small farmers need cooperative action at all levels—in purchasing, marketing, and sharing of equipment—to achieve economies not available to them as individuals. In the past there has been surprisingly little sharing of equipment among farmers—even of costly machinery used one week a year.

The problems of the farm worker displaced by mechanization have been addressed from various points of view. Cesar Chavez, speaking to the University of California Board of Regents said, "Our union does not oppose progress . . . we do not even oppose mechanization . . . But we believe the progress should be complete. The other half of the job is to use this improved technology to develop complementary programs for the workers who are losing their jobs. Research should benefit everyone, workers as well as growers." Recent efforts at helping farm workers help themselves have resulted in such triumphs as the Cooperativa Campesino in Watsonville and the Cooperative Central in Salinas, California, where former farm worker families—the poorest of all farmers—joined to grow strawberries on land leased from the county by local non-profit organizations, competing successfully with the state's large corporate growers and earning a great deal more money by their own efforts than they had as employees.

Black landowners, virtually all of whom have been small farmers, are losing their farms at a rate three times that of the national average. Whereas 15 million acres of land in the U.S. were owned by blacks in 1910, 6 million were still held by black families in a 1970 survey. A major problem in black farm ownership has been legal entanglements, which have made it impossible to obtain clear title to land. When ownership records are incomplete and, therefore, title to a piece of land is unclear, the land cannot be mortgaged or used as collateral for loans for equipment or any other legitimate purpose. Poor black farmers have traditionally neglected to leave wills, and properties are inherited by numerous family members in far-flung communities.

A typical story is that of the Boles family, who live on land

119

in Beaufort County, South Carolina, purchased by John Boles, their grandfather who, as a freedman, bought ten acres from a local planter. John Boles received title to the land, planted it in vegetables and cotton, and died in 1915 leaving three sons. As was common, he wrote no will so the land was inherited by the three sons equally. Two sons migrated to New York and one continued to work the land until 1950 when he passed it on to one of his sons, who has been farming it since and living in the deteriorating farmhouse his grandfather built in 1865. When the family applied under a government program of the Farmer's Home Administration for help in building a new house he was told he needed "quit claim" deeds from all relatives having an interest in the ten acres. He was able to acquire signatures from all except one uncle whose whereabouts was unknown to any family member. This "missing interest" made him ineligible for the assistance he sought and also ineligible for standard bank loans.

Two southern states, South Carolina and Mississippi, are considering bills to assist black farmers with their expensive and complex legal problems. A completely different effort to help small farmers is focused on enforcement of the 1902 Reclamation Act which specified that in Federal reclamation projects in seventeen western states ownership should be restricted to 160 acres of federally irrigated land per person. The law also said that farmers receiving federal water must live on or near their land. At the time, Theodore Roosevelt announced: "Money is being spent to build up the little man of the West so that no big man from east or west can come in to get a monopoly on the water."

In restricting the size of individual holdings and requiring residence, the obvious intent of the law was to open the land to settlement by family-sized farms. However, as with the Homestead Act, the law was not enforced and has been flagrantly violated. The most controversial districts are in the Central Valley area of California. In California's Imperial Valley, 70 percent of the land is held in vast tracts by large growers, agribusiness corporations, and other absentees.

In the 1970s a group of California activists interested in land reform started an organization named National Lands for

120

People and led the fight to enforce the original rulings and intent of the 1902 act. As the result of their lawsuit, in 1977 the courts directed the Secretary of the Interior to enforce the law, and new rules and regulations and amendments should be completed by July 1981 in accordance with the results of an Environmental Impact Statement now in progress. The Secretary of the Interior has stated that any amendments to the law should reflect the original purpose—to provide family farms and to spread the benefits of the Federal investment to as many people as possible.

The National Family Farm Coalition, centered in Washington, D.C., is promoting the passage of a Family Farm Development Act in the belief that "protecting America's family farmers is the most effective way to create a self-sustaining, environmentally sound, economically stable food system." They are effectively disputing—through educational programs and lobbying—the view that family farmers are inefficient, demonstrating that tax laws, the targeting of government programs, and the focus of research have brought about their decline.

The proposed Family Farm Development Act would set up a Federally funded direct marketing system in an attempt to bring farmers and consumers together again—for the benefit of both. The farmer, who brought his goods to town to sell to city folk, began losing contact with buyers in the mid-nineteenth century when he started selling at wholesale prices to an expanding chain of distributors, processors, retailers, and other middle-men, who now receive 61 cents of each dollar spent on food in this country.

The direct marketing approach involves "Buy Local" campaigns involving labeling, publicity, and promotion. These are currently in effect in several states. In California you can dial a toll-free number and get the latest information on farms in your area that are selling fruits or vegetables or inviting you to "pick-your-own" in their fields.

The Greenmarket, organized by the Council of the Environment of New York City, is a highly successful project, which is being studied by other urban areas. The Greenmarket opened in 1976 and is held at eight different urban sites enabling farmers, who bring their produce in from relatively nearby rural areas, to realize substantial profits while providing consumers with fresh produce during the growing season.

In Boston, Louisville, Syracuse, Santa Fe, Honolulu, San Jose, Pittsburgh, Birmingham, Detroit, Nashville, and other cities new farmers' markets are proving successful. In the town of Las Cruces, New Mexico, in the south central part of the state, the market takes place on a downtown mall given by the city for market use on Wednesdays and Saturdays. Started by a local doctor, the League of Women Voters, and representatives from the city, the market offers space to farmers, to backyard growers from town, to children from 4-H, Future Farmers of America, and Scouting organizations.

In Boston, the 150 year old Quincy Market near historic Faneuil Hall has been hailed not only as a very successful merchandising project but as one of the most innovative urban renewal projects ever undertaken. In West Virginia, a pioneering program begun in the 1940s and financed with help from both state and Federal funds now operates markets in six different cities. In Pennsylvania, state-sponsored "tail-gate" markets have been a notable success and the state also publishes directories of farmer-to-consumer merchandising opportunities. These new farmers' markets and other city markets that survive from earlier times, as well as a proliferation of roadside country stands, find enthusiastic acceptance from young people exposed to food marketing since infancy from a seat in a cart at the orderly, odorless supermarket. Young adults, who as children believed that carrots had no tops and that lettuce grew wrapped in cellophane and that home baked bread and home preserves were items great grandma enjoyed because she had no alternative, throng to the produce markets happily smelling, pinching, and tasting. They rush to the country on fine days to avail themselves of "pick-your-own" offers. The farmer, who saves the cost of harvesting, and the consumer, who has a fine day and takes home bushels of fresh inexpensive fruits and vegetables have, in their joint enthusiasm, made a great success of an obvious but relatively new marketing idea.

If you ask the man or woman picking strawberries or selecting perfect tomatoes from a bin on a busy New York street

122

The Greenmarket in New York City. © STEVEN L. BORNS 1979

whether it is important that the family farm survive you'll receive a strong affirmative. Ask the farmer selling the tomatoes and his response will be the same. If pressed for reasons both might respond in a way cynics would call sentimental. The small farmer is the true American, they might say, whether or not they read Jefferson, and the rural landscape provides our most beautiful scenery. The farmer, they might add, lives a healthy independent life close to the earth. His children grow up surrounded by the beauty and fascination of the natural world instead of the decay and vice of the city. They learn in a natural fashion about life and death and reproduction; they learn about responsibility and about work and its rewards. And although the deprivations of small farm life are recognized and although in recent decades country people have become a good bit more like city people in their tastes and expectations, essentially what is said by farm people and by wistful urbanites about the benefits of a rural environment still rings true. We expect people from the country to be more virtuous than city people for just these reasons.

In his book, *Farm Boy,* which explores the lives and feelings of three generations of farmers in Illinois, Archie Lieberman presents the young farmer, Bill Hammer, Jr., speaking of growing up on the farm:

> It was fun learning to do things I saw him [his father] do, to respect him and what he was doing, and I'd want to learn the job, too. Then the day came when he'd let me do something. Then in a year I'd be a little older and he'd start me in on something new. It was a joy learning and thinking that you're a man before you really are . . . I had friends, other kids around the country. But Dad was my best friend.

Looking back through our history, it becomes obvious that farmers still like farming for the same old reasons. They treasure the freedom to make their own decisions, to manage their own place. They like working out of doors. They want to bring up their children in the environment they consider most healthy and satisfying. In exchange for providing food and fiber in

124

abundance they ask for an income that will provide a standard of living equivalent to that of Americans in other occupations.

A current back-to-the-land movement testifies to the fact that more and more men and women, most of them from non-farm backgrounds, now prefer country life. Since 1970 the tide of movement from country to city which population experts considered unalterable has been reversed and our major population growth has been in rural areas. Seventeen rural states: Maine, Minnesota, Iowa, North Dakota, South Dakota, Nebraska, North Carolina, South Carolina, Kansas, Tennessee, Alabama, Arkansas, Montana, Idaho, Wyoming, New Mexico, and Utah have, since 1970 grown in population, with most migrants coming from urban areas. Seven predominantly urban states have lost population.

Helen and Scott Nearing, now aged seventy-five and ninety-six, left the city and returned to the land fifty years ago and their experiences with subsistence organic farming in Vermont and Maine are chronicled in their books, *Living the Good Life* and *Continuing the Good Life.* They have received, through the years, thousands of visitors seeking instruction and inspiration for their own endeavors in self-sufficient living. Many young people in New England and in other parts of the country have drawn confidence and practical guidance from the experiences of the Nearings and have been able to establish successful small farming ventures of their own. Substituting their labor for mechanized techniques and organic methods for chemicals they have, by reverting to older methods of farming, been able to survive on the land and fulfill emotional and spiritual needs. Some of the most passionately committed young farmers are, like the Nearings, men and women from urban backgrounds.

Newcomers to rural areas speak of the better quality of life available in the country, the independence of rural people, the beauty of the land. They understand those who have written about the farmer's almost mystical attachment to the land, which has been eloquently expressed throughout our history.

In 1889 Samuel Guard, editor of the *Breeder's Gazette* started each issue with this observation: "The farmer is a believer.

Idaho farmer using a snowmobile to check his cattle. UNITED STATES DEPARTMENT OF AGRICULTURE *(following page)*

Naturally a believer. He plows in faith; he sows in hope; he reaps in charity." In Archie Lieberman's *Farm Boy* a cousin of the Hammers' says:

> I have a different feeling of what it means to love the land than what someone else might have. To me the land is my being. It's all I've got. It's my existence . . . I feel like I'm just a part of it; and when you read in the Bible where it says God gave you this land to till it, to take care of it, to prosper, that's what it means to me. That is my duty to do this. I don't consider it a job exactly. It's a duty. A responsibility. That gives me my happiness and satisfaction and a reason for being here.

The poet-farmer Wendell Berry reminds us that "agriculture" properly means not growing crops, but cultivating the land, and that "cultivation" refers not only to tillage but to "cult" or worship. The small farmer, he points out, cares about the land and is intent on preserving this treasure for future generations. True efficiency, he tells us, "is neither cheap (in terms of skill and labor) nor fast. Real efficiency is long-term efficiency. It is to be found in means that are in keeping with and preserving of their ends, in methods of production that preserve the sources of production . . ."

A great many of the hardheaded economists, government planners, and agricultural policy makers are now in agreement with poets, tillers, and environmentalists about the importance of saving the family farm. They do not consider nostalgia an appropriate basis for government policy, but for the most practical reasons—fear of energy shortages, unalterable pollution, decay of rural economies—they are hitting hard at the old belief that farmers only succeed by getting big. President Richard Nixon's Secretary of Agriculture Earl Butz warned the small farmers of America to "get big or get out." Now Department of Agriculture spokesmen insist that, on the basis of a number of careful studies, the family farm is the most efficient unit of production when judged by the true measure of efficiency: output per unit of input.

One recent Department report concluded: "We are so conditioned to equate bigness with efficiency that nearly everyone

128

assumes that large-scale undertakings are inherently more efficient than smaller ones. In fact, the claim of efficiency is commonly used to justify bigness. But when we examine the realities we find that most of the economies associated with size in farming are achieved by the one or two man fully mechanized farm."

Currently, the average size of a corporate vegetable farm in California is 3,206 acres, whereas the Department of Agriculture found that the optimum size in terms of the best return on the amount of energy expended for a California vegetable farm would be 440 acres.

Studies of the financial distress afflicting many large corporate farms emphasize the small farmer's intimate involvement with the property he owns and loves and depends on for a living. "Who will sit up with the corporate sow?" is the title of one investigation. Another recent article on financial losses sustained by farms run by hired managers quotes an old saying, which holds that profitable farming results from "the shadow of the owner on the land." In addressing the National Press Club in Washington, D.C. Secretary of Agriculture Bergland favored the footprint rather than the shadow, saying, "Someone once said that the best fertilizer one can put on the soil of a farm is the footprint of the owner, and I've seen plenty of evidence that this is true."

The family farm is not an inefficient outmoded institution but a vital small-scale capitalistic and competitive enterprise currently in crisis due to public policies that have encouraged bigness. The strength of the family farmer is his resilience. In a bad year the large corporate farm, which has high fixed costs for needed labor, may go under. The family farmer, who is self-employed and who has the motivation only the owner can have, pulls in his belt, lives on less, postpones new purchases and maintenance costs, works as many hours as the job requires, supervised only by himself, stays attentive to the health of his animals and his crop. The family farmer, who can do without, who can improvise, remains at the heart of the food production system despite falling markets, bad weather, and other hardships he cannot control.

Without radical changes in public policy the trend toward

129

consolidation of farmland will continue and the number of farmers will wane. Lawrence Higbee in a study for the Twentieth Century Fund titled *Farms and Farmers in an Urban Age* wrote:

> Less thought has been given to the problem of surplus men than to that of surplus crops. More anxiety has been expressed over price supports for milk than over how to get these surpluses consumed by people who need milk but cannot afford it. Abuses of acreage allotment privileges and scandalous grain storage operations have aroused public indignation, but the plight of disrupted lives has been accepted apathetically.

We are learning today that maintaining our high level of agricultural production does not have to mean that over one hundred thousand farmers a year become surplus citizens and that the disappearance of rural and small town America is not a historic inevitability. Belief that there should be freedom of entry into useful occupations means that careers in farming should be a realistic aspiration for young people, poor people, minority people.

Can we save the family farm? Perhaps the most useful answer is another question: Can we afford to permit it to die?

Suggestions for Further Reading

AGEE, James and EVANS, Walker. *Let Us Now Praise Famous Men*
Text and photographs on conditions in the rural south in the 1930s

BERRY, Wendell. *The Unsettling of America:* Culture and Agriculture
Essays by an idealistic poet-farmer.

CARSON, Rachel. *Silent Spring*
Pesticides and our natural environment

CATHER, Willa. *My Antonia*
Novel about a family of Bohemian settlers in Nebraska

CONRAT, Maisie and CONRAT, Richard. *The American Farm*
A photographic history of American agriculture

CREWES, Harry. *A Childhood*
Recollections of a grim childhood in the rural south

FITE, Gilbert. *The Farmers' Frontier: 1865–1900*
History of the movement westward in the post Civil War period.

GREENBERG, David B., ed. *Land That Our Fathers Plowed: The Settlement of Our Country as Told by the Pioneers Themselves and Their Contemporaries*
Short selections dating from colonial days to the closing of the frontier

LIEBERMAN, Archie. *Farm Boy*
Photographic record of three generations of farmers in the Midwest

MERRILL, Richard, editor. *Radical Agriculture*
Collection of pieces on recent controversial agricultural issues

MORROW, Wilson and Fremon, Suzanne, eds. *Rural America*
Selection of writings on today's agricultural scene

NEARING, Scott and Nearing, Helen. *Living the Good Life* and *Continuing the Good Life*
Contemporary subsistence farmers and their experiences on the land in Vermont and Maine

RASMUSSEN, Wayne David. *Readings in the History of American Agriculture*
Fifty-two selections highlighting landmark events in American agriculture

RUSSELL, Howard. *Long Deep Furrow:* Three Centuries of Farming in New England

STAMPP, Kenneth M. *Peculiar Institution:* Slavery in the Ante-Bellum South

STEINBECK, John. *The Grapes of Wrath*
Novel about a family of tenant farmers from a dust bowl region of Oklahoma who travel to California to find work

TAYLOR, Ronald B. *Chavez and the Farm Workers*

USDA YEARBOOKS.
Annual publications of the Department of Agriculture. Each issue focuses on a particular agricultural subject. Issues from many years can be found in most public libraries

Index

acreage allotment payments, 88
acreage retirement, 89-90, 111
Agee, James, 92-94
Agent Orange, 15
agribusiness, 102, 106-107; vs. family farm, 115-116, 128-129
Agricultural Act, 110-111
Agricultural Adjustment Acts, 87-89
Agricultural Adjustment Administration, 94, 96
Agricultural Office, 79
agricultural societies, 64-66
Agriculture Department, 14, 16, 18-20, 46, 78-80, 83; and family farm, 114-115, 116, 128, 129; in 1930s, 87, 88
Allen, Frederick Lewis, 97
American Agricultural Movement, 113
American Farm Bureau, 85
The American Farmer, 66
American Friends Service, 46

back-to-the-land movement, 125
Bank for Cooperatives, 118
barter, 30
Benton, Thomas Hart, 57
Bergland, Robert, 129
Berkshire Agricultural Society, 66
Berry, Wendell, 128
blacks: and family farm, 119-120; farm organizations, 78; migration, post-WWI, 86; in 1930s, 94-96; and sharecropping, 42-43; and western settlement, 57
Boles, John, 119-120

boll weevil, 80
Boone, Daniel, 51
bracero program, 46-48
Bryan, William Jennings, 78
Butz, Earl, 11, 128

Caldwell, Erskine, 92
Cannon, Joseph, 19
Carson, Rachel, 14
Chavez, Cesar, 119
Civilian Conservation Corps, 100
Colored Farmer's National Alliance and Cooperative Union, 78
Columbian Agricultural Society, 64-66
combines, 74
Commodity Credit Corp., 88
Common Cause, 117
common land, 50
conservation, 19-20
contract farming, 107
Cooperativa Campesino, 119
Cooperative Central, 119
cooperatives, 82, 118-119
corn, 26, 68-69; hybrid, 100
corporate farming, *see* agribusiness
costs, 104, 108-109; WWI, 83-86
cotton, 32, 80, 82, 87, 90; and slavery, 38-40
Council of the Environment of New York City, 121-122
county extension system, 80
county fairs, 64, 66
credit, 108-109, 118
Crewes, Harry, 94
crop rotation, 15, 29-30

DDT, 12-15
Deane, Samuel, 32
Deere, John, 74
DES (diethylstilbesterol) , 17-18
Domestic Allotment Act, 88
dry farming, 61
dust bowl, 96-97

efficiency, farms, 128-129
Eisenhower, Dwight D., 110
Eliot, Jared, 22, 32
electricity, 89
employment, off-farm, 8, 108
energy, 11-12, 116
Environmental Protection Agency, 12, 14
Evans, George Henry, 56
Evans, Walker, 92

family farm, 33; decline of, 101-112; saving, 113-130
Family Farm Development Act, 121
farm (s) : number, 7, 100, 101; population, 8, 78, 86; size, 7, 28, 100, 129; value, 108-109; workers, 33-48, 119; *see also* family farm; migratory workers; sharecroppers
Farm Act (1977) , 111
Farm Boy, 124, 128
Farm Bureau, 113
farmers, 3, 104-106
Farmers' Alliances, 78
Farmer's Home Administration, 20, 116, 120
farmers' markets, 121-123
Farmer's Union, 85
Farm Journal, 117
Farm Security Administration, 89, 92, 118
fertilizer, 8, 12, 17-18, 76
flooding, 100
Food and Agriculture Act, 19-20
Food and Drug Administration, 14
fruits, 10-11, 70

Garland, Hamlin, 68-69
girdling, 22
government farm policies, 83, 86-100, 115-129
Graham Experimental Farm and Training Center, 118-119
Grange, 76-78, 85, 113
grasshoppers, 57-60
Greenmarket, 121-122, 123
Guard, Samuel, 125-126

Hatch Act (1887) , 79-80
Hawthorne, Nathaniel, 63
herbicides, 12, 15
Hessian fly, 16, 64
Higbee, Lawrence, 130
hogs, 69
Homestead Act, 42, 54, 56, 60-61, 120
homesteaders, 56-62
houses, 28, 30, 64, 89

income, farms, 86, 87, 89, 92, 100; and bigness, 101, 107, 113
indentured servants, 34-35, 49
Indians, 21-24, 37, 61-62
indigo, 32, 38
insecticides, 12-16, 48
Integrated Pest Management, 15, 16
investment, foreign, 115

Jamestown, 24, 36
Jefferson, Thomas, 3, 6, 29-30, 32
Jones, Donald, 100
journals for farmers, 1800s, 66

Kelly, Oliver, 76
Klamath weed, 16

land: distribution, 49-62; family vs. corporate farming, 101-102, 106, 108-109, 111-112; foreign investment in, 115; movement back to, 125; reform, 120-121; speculation in, 50, 54; and tax laws, 117

land grant, 51; college, 79
land rush, 62
Lieberman, Archie, 124, 128
life expectancy, farm workers, 48
Lincoln, Abraham, 56, 77
literacy, 30-32, 66
loans, 88, 118

machinery, 74-76, 108-109
magazines for farmers, 66
manufacturing vs. agriculture, 10
marketing, direct, 121-123
McCormick, Cyrus, 74
meat packing, 69, 70
mechanization, 7-11, 74-76, 100, 119
migratory worker, 8, 11, 34, 43-48
Minnesota Family Farm Security Act
    (1976), 118
Missouri Small Farm Program, 116
Morrill Land Grant Act (1862), 79

National Farmer's Organization, 113
National Farmer's Union, 113
National Labor Relations Act, 46
National Lands for People, 120-121
National Reclamation Act (1902),
    19
National Sharecroppers' Fund, 96,
    118-119
Nearing, Scott and Helen, 125
Nelson, Gaylord, 118
New Deal, 87-100, 118
Newton, Isaac, 21
The New York Farmer, 66

Office of Economic Opportunity, 118
Oklahoma: dust storms, 96-97; home-
    steaders, 61-62
organic farming, 17, 18
organizations, farm, 76-79

parity policy, 88-89, 100
pest control, biological, 15-17
pesticides, 12-16, 48

Philadelphia Society for Promoting
    Agriculture, 64
The Ploughboy, 66
plows, 25, 74
Pocahontas, 25
Populist party, 79
prices, 7, 86-87, 111
price supports, 19, 88, 109-112, 113
productivity, 7-8, 76
public domain, 49-62

railroads, 54-56, 70-74
reaper, 74
Reclamation Act (1902), 120
research, 10-11, 112, 116
Resettlement Administration, 89
rice, and slavery, 38
Rolfe, John, 24
Roosevelt, Franklin D., 87
Roosevelt, Theodore, 19, 120
Royal Africa Company, 38
Rural Electrification Act (1935), 89
Rural Training, Research, and Dem-
    onstration Farming Center, 118
Rusk, Jeremiah, 80

sharecroppers, 34, 42-43, 89-97
slavery, 34-42
Small Business Administration, 20
Smith, Adam, 10
Smith Lever Act, 80
smoking, 35-36
soil: erosion and conservation, 18-20,
    29, 100; tillage, 15
Soil Conservation Act, 88
Soil Conservation Service, 18, 100
The Southern Agriculturist, 63, 66
Southern Cooperative Development
    Fund, 118
Southern Regional Council, 118
Southern Tenant Farmers Union, 94
specialization, 68, 76, 101
Steinbeck, John, 90, 97
surplus, 8, 21, 87-88, 100

Swanson, Louise, 103
Swift, Jonathan, 21

taxes, 106, 111-112, 116-118
tenant farmers, 43, 83, 89-97
Tennessee Valley Authority, 100
Terkel, Studs, 112
Thomas, Norman, 96
threshers, 74
tobacco, 24, 30, 32, 35,40, 82
Tocqueville, Alexis de, 64
tomatoes, 10-11, 112
tools, 24-25, 74

trade, 28-29, 82, 86
transportation, 28-29, 54-56, 70-74

United Farm Workers, 48
vegetables, 10-11

Wallace, Henry A., 87
Washington, George, 29-30, 64
water pollution and fertilizers, 17
Webster, Noah, 32
wheat, 68-69, 76, 87, 113
women, and taxes, 117-118